THE UNIVERSITY OF NORTH CAROLINA
SESQUICENTENNIAL PUBLICATIONS

UNIVERSITY EXTENSION IN ACTION

THE UNIVERSITY OF NORTH CAROLINA
SESQUICENTENNIAL PUBLICATIONS

Louis R. Wilson, DIRECTOR

CHRONICLES OF THE SESQUICENTENNIAL

THE UNIVERSITY OF NORTH CAROLINA, 1789-1835:
A DOCUMENTARY HISTORY

THE CAMPUS OF THE FIRST STATE UNIVERSITY

THE GRADUATE SCHOOL: RESEARCH AND PUBLICATIONS

THE GRADUATE SCHOOL: DISSERTATIONS AND THESES

STUDIES IN SCIENCE

STUDIES IN LANGUAGE AND LITERATURE

A HUNDRED YEARS OF LEGAL EDUCATION

A STATE UNIVERSITY SURVEYS THE HUMANITIES

SECONDARY EDUCATION IN THE SOUTH

IN SEARCH OF THE REGIONAL BALANCE OF AMERICA

STUDIES IN HISTORY AND POLITICAL SCIENCE

LIBRARY RESOURCES OF THE UNIVERSITY OF NORTH CAROLINA

RESEARCH AND REGIONAL WELFARE

PIONEERING A PEOPLE'S THEATER

UNIVERSITY EXTENSION IN ACTION

BOOKS FROM CHAPEL HILL

UNIVERSITY EXTENSION IN ACTION

RUSSELL M. GRUMMAN
Director, University Extension Division

With the Collaboration of

C. E. McINTOSH, ROY W. MORRISON
AGATHA BOYD ADAMS, REX WINSLOW
KATHERINE JOCHER, ALBERT COATES
S. E. LEAVITT AND T. J. WILSON

CHAPEL HILL
THE UNIVERSITY OF NORTH CAROLINA PRESS

1947

Copyright, 1947, by
THE UNIVERSITY OF NORTH CAROLINA PRESS

Printed in the United States of America by
The Orange Printshop

FOREWORD

The term "University Extension" in the title is understood to include, as nearly as possible, all of the extra-mural services and activities of the University. Since the University Extension Division has been responsible for the major portion of these action programs, the account herewith presented is unintentionally, but nevertheless quite naturally, overweighted with the story of extension as formally organized and recognized at the University.

The services of the University are actually being "extended" in countless ways and in many directions. Hence it would be impracticable, if not impossible, to be all-inclusive in this volume. Chapter VI presents briefly the work of several University organizations that are considered to be important agencies of University Extension and adult education. The Extension Division maintains a close working relationship with practically all of these organizations so that there exists, in effect, coordination of effort in University Extension and cooperation within the University, which are regarded as essential characteristics of good administration.

The University of North Carolina is traditionally committed to an expanding program of University Extension. It is to be sincerely hoped that this volume may assist in evaluating the institution's effort and help lay the foundation for intelligent planning and development of University services to all of the people of North Carolina.

The author wishes to acknowledge with great appreciation and sincere thanks the assistance of the collaborators who contributed chapters and articles as follows: C. E. McIntosh, Historical Background; Roy W. Morrison, Special Aspects of Extra-mural In-service Teacher Education; Agatha Boyd

FOREWORD

Adams, Library Extension Service and War Information Center; Rex Winslow, Bureau of Business Services and Research; Katherine Jocher, Institute for Research in Social Science; Albert Coates, Institute of Government; Sturgis E. Leavitt, Inter-American Institute; and Thomas J. Wilson, University of North Carolina Press.

The author is indebted also to the Director of the Sesquicentennial Publications, Dr. Louis R. Wilson, who has been extremely helpful in planning the book and in supplying data from his experience and long connection with the University.

If a dedication were in order it would be made, with humble thanks, to the author's wife, Vida Church Grumman, who carried the major part of the load of assembling the material and of writing the preliminary drafts of most sections of the book not listed above.

University Extension in Action was first prepared as a bulletin of the University Extension Division and is published here as the contribution of the University Extension Division to the Sesquicentennial Celebration of the University as one of the Sesquicentennial Publications.

Chapel Hill, N. C. R. M. G.
July 1, 1946

CONTENTS

	Page
Foreword	iii
Introduction	1

I
HISTORICAL BACKGROUND
C. E. McIntosh, *Acting Head, Bureau of High School Relations*

The Beginnings of University Extension	13
The Faculty Committee	15
The Bureau of Extension	16
The University Extension Division	18
The Directorate of Extension	21

II
TEACHING SERVICES

Extension Class Instruction	25
Correspondence Instruction	28
Special Aspects of Extra-Mural In-service Teacher Education (Roy W. Morrison, *Professor of Education*)	30
Post-Graduate Medical and Dental Courses	39
Short Courses and Institutes	42
Study Tours	48

III
LIBRARY EXTENSION SERVICE
Agatha Boyd Adams, *Associate Head, Library Extension Department*

Library Extension Service	51

IV

SCHOOL AND COMMUNITY ACTIVITIES

	Page
Art	59
Audio-Visual Education	62
Debating, Athletic, and Academic Contests	65
Drama	67
English	71
Lectures and Lecture Courses	74
Music	75
Public Forums	77
Publicaitons	78
Radio	82
Recreation	85

V

COOPERATION WITH STATE, REGIONAL, AND NATIONAL ORGANIZATIONS

State Organizations	93
North Carolina Congress of Parents and Teachers	93
North Carolina State Board of Health	96
North Carolina State Department of Public Instruction	97
Regional Organizations	100
Southern Council on International Relations	101
National Organizations	102

VI

UNIVERSITY AGENCIES OF ADULT EDUCATION

The Bureau of Business Services and Research (Rex Winslow, *Director*)	109

	Page
The Folklore Council	110
The Institute for Research in Social Science (Katherine Jocher, *Assistant Director*)	111
The Institute of Government (Albert Coates, *Director*)	119
The Inter-American Institute (Sturgis E. Leavit, *Director*)	125
The University of North Carolina Press (Thomas J. Wilson, *Director*)	129

VII

A LOOK AHEAD

The Communication Center	160
Workers Education	160
Cultural and Recreational Life	162
Adult Education—Leadership and Teaching Materials	162
Research Interpretation	163
"All-University" Extension	165
Index	169

UNIVERSITY EXTENSION IN ACTION

INTRODUCTION

With few exceptions, the University Extension Division serves as the administrative agency through which are conducted the extension activities of the University of North Carolina at Chapel Hill. In carrying out this function, the Division endeavors to work cooperatively with all departments, schools, and other University organizations. Therefore, in reviewing the major extension activities of the past thirty-four years, credit for successful achievements is shared by administrative officials, faculty members, and members of the Extension Division staff. The record is impressive, perhaps, from the viewpoint of variety and scope of University service to the State. It gives emphasis to the fact that the University of North Carolina is "The University of the People."

Since the activities and services are not easily arranged chronologically, they have been classified for presentation under six headings. Space permits only brief statements about the extension services included in this review. The story is incomplete, but it is hoped that it is sufficiently comprehensive to give a fair picture of University Extension in action at the University of North Carolina.

It may be truly said that citizens of North Carolina look to the University as their institution and turn to it for information, inspiration, and leadership. Hence the pattern of University Extension has been shaped very largely by the demands made upon the University by the people. Citizens of the State have every reason to expect their State University (created and supported by them) to be democratic and to serve their social, economic, intellectual, and cultural interests. This is the task and the special responsibility of the University Extension Division. The work of the Division, therefore, includes the planning, organization, promotion, and administration of general adult educational activities, public relations, and service projects. Internally, it is organized into a small number of bureaus to facilitate this work for the University. The University, through the Extension Division, has been an active member of the National University Extension Association, since the Association was established in 1915. An Administrative Board composed of several deans and faculty members advises the Director in matters of general policy.

The University Goes to the People

The original slogan of the University Extension Division, "The State is the Campus," has become a reality. From Manteo to Murphy, in every county and in every community, the University has literally gone to the people. By means of home study courses, library service, extension classes, lectures, the *University of North Carolina News Letter*, radio programs, recreational and cultural activities, the campus of the University of North Carolina has become coterminous with the boundaries of the Commonwealth. Thus, the facilities and services of the University continuously flow to the people in an ever-widening stream. Actually the requests for educational services are, at times, greater than the ability of the University to meet them, *i.e.*, in terms of personnel and financial resources. Those persons receiving formal extension instruction are quite willing to pay the nominal fees charged (usually determined on a cost basis). But most of the non-credit or informal types of adult education such as radio programs, public forums, and lectures, are non-revenue producing activities; therefore, such services must be subsidized by the State. It has been the policy of the Division to initiate programs of information, training, and education of interest to the general public. These frequently result in requests from individuals and organizations for more specific reading or study courses to meet their particular needs.

The People Come to the University

The interchange between the University and the people operates on the campus at Chapel Hill as well as on the state-wide campus. Within recent years with the addition of The Carolina Inn, The Institute of Government building, and improved housing and eating facilities on the campus and in the community, there has developed a new trend in University Extension—the coming of the people to the University for meetings, conferences, short courses, institutes, clinics, symposia, and other forms of education for part-time students. Several of these activities have become annual events. Some people come for the professional development to be gained through refresher courses; others, as members of state organizations interested in special programs of education; still others come simply for "the sake of learning."

The University of North Carolina has become known as an intellectual and cultural center. As such it seeks to share that distinction and that responsible opportunity with the people of the region and nation. In Chapter VI it will be seen that this function has also been extended to the peoples of Latin American countries and to those from other parts of the world.

People come to the campus to attend a lecture or a concert, to visit Person Hall Art Gallery, to witness a performance by The Carolina Playmakers, or to see a football game; but they also come to stay several days or even six to eight weeks to attend some course or institute. Since 1935, The Extension Division has served as the administrative agency, working in cooperation with academic departments and schools, responsible for making and handling all local arrangements, including housing and financial, in connection with group visitations of all kinds. Many of these activities are referred to in Chapters II and V. In the main they represent a cooperative educational endeavor between the University, on the one hand, and associations of people, on the other.

It should be emphasized that the Extension Division works very closely and cooperatively with the Summer Session in sponsoring and conducting the special programs for adults held during the summer months. At that time, more visiting groups can usually be accommodated and served by the faculty. It should also be pointed out that visiting instructors are frequently employed when needed to supplement the regular staff.

The University and the Public Schools

President Frank P. Graham had this to say about "The Schools of the People" in his inaugural address, delivered November 11, 1931: "The public schools are now and will increasingly be the community center of university extension and adult education. The University will not only extend and share its life with the public schools and the people but University men ... will fight for the schools of the people. ... The University is resourced in the public schools and the public schools are resourced in the University. They go up or down together."

This statement expresses the spirit of the historical relationship between the University and public education in North Carolina. It also voices the underlying philosophy of the longstanding policy of the University with respect to this phase of University Extension. With the possible exception of library extension service (although even this began as a supplementary aid to schools), extension activities and services with the public schools have been the most consistent and far-reaching of all extension work thus far. The first organized effort on the part of the University along this line was the formation in 1912 of the

INTRODUCTION 5

North Carolina High School Debating Union, simultaneously with the organization of the Bureau of Extension. High School relations have since been developed to include athletics, dramatic art, music, graphic arts, English, academic contests, student government, and journalism. In practically every case, these activities have been conducted as a means of assisting the schools with their regular or extracurricular programs and to provide impetus, stimulation, leadership, and direction to them. In most of this work, there was no other state agency available to undertake it, and there have been many instances in which the University has been requested to assume the responsibility. As the pattern of public education in North Carolina changes so the plan and scope of extension activities in this field must change. Such adjustments, to conform with modern practices and principles of education, are not only incumbent upon the University, they should emanate from it as a natural part of its leadership of education.

The most important and the most effective phase of University Extension relationship to public education in North Carolina has been the program of in-service teacher education. Working in close affiliation with the State Department of Public Instruction, the North Carolina Education Association, the North Carolina College Conference, and the University departments concerned, the Extension Division has made a real contribution to the improvement of classroom instruction, supervision, and the administration of schools. Indirectly, but no less effective, has been the cooperative work with the North Carolina Congress of Parents and Teachers that has resulted in better understanding of and many improvements in the school program. Public opinion based upon an intelligent understanding of education leads in most instances to constructive school legislation and public support. This has been and should continue to be one of the purposes of University Extension as it relates to public education.

The University and Adult Education

One of the chief functions of the University Extension Division has been to promote and conduct educational programs for adults and to train adult education teachers and leaders. Most of the activities and services of the Division may be classified as forms of adult education. University Extension has become recognized as one of the leading agencies in North Carolina for the development of the intellectual, cultural, and recreational life of the adult citizens of the State.

The term, "Adult Education," in North Carolina no longer suggests an educational program confined to adult illiterates but implies and includes instruction and all other kinds of educational opportunity for out-of-school youth, as well as for adults regardless of their social, economic, or academic status. Such an interpretation of adult education suggests an all-inclusive, comprehensive program as the objective of the Extension Division. Thus the University has attempted to implement this idea by working with any group in the State and with regional and national organizations interested in adult educational programs.

Students of adult education including visitors from several foreign countries have come to Chapel Hill to observe University Extension in action.

University leadership has made contributions to the development of the adult education movement not only in North Carolina but also in the South and in the nation. Notable, too, have been recent efforts and programs of adult education in Inter-American and International Relations.

Many new programs of adult education are being developed with which the University of North Carolina will continue to play a leading role. It has a unique opportunity and responsibility, as a state agency, to train leaders and to direct the education of adults.

INTRODUCTION

University Extension in Wartime

The pattern of University Extension during the war emergency, 1941-1945, was quite similar to that during 1917-1918. In each of these war periods, the University made major adjustments to serve the nation. Extension services were likewise changed to meet the needs of the times.

During World War I, the Bureau of Extension was very active in publishing and distributing literature, in sending lecturers to communities throughout the State, and otherwise leading the wartime thinking and discussion of North Carolinians.

Before Pearl Harbor, the Extension Division served as the coordinating agency of the University's Center for Civilian Morale Service. This led to the organization of the War Information Center at the University Library which served both the campus and the State.

The organization of federal agencies such as the Office of War Information, the Office of Price Administration, War Manpower Commission, Engineering, Science, and Management War Training, United States Armed Forces Institute, and others gave the University many new avenues of extension service during World War II. Participation of the University of North Carolina in these services is described briefly in Chapter VII.

Other adjustments to wartime conditions were, of course, necessary, including the modification of the regularly established extension services. Administrative, financial, and personnel problems were pyramided in the attempt to keep alive essential activities in addition to the new activities more directly related to the war effort.

University Extension Tomorrow

Solid foundations have been laid for the future expansion and development of University Extension at the University of North Carolina. A sound philosophy underlies and supports the idea that, along with teaching and research, one of the major functions of the modern state university is extension.

University Extension in North Carolina in the future will depend upon intelligent planning and imaginative leadership. It, too, will be necessarily limited by the resources and wealth of the State which it should indirectly help to create. Within the University itself, University Extension should expect to receive an equitable share of state appropriations in order to carry out the essential features of its function and responsibility to the people of the State. Financial subsidy of extension services should not, however, be permitted to jeopardize or to curtail the resident functions of the University. Since many extension activities produce revenue and others may be financed partially or wholly through grants, it may be assumed that no serious administrative problem or policy is involved that would effect plans for expansion.

In Chapter VIII an attempt has been made to outline the trend of University Extension in North Carolina. Some of the developments mentioned are already well underway, such as the Communication Center, and the services to business, industry, and to organized labor. Part-time educational programs for veterans will unquestionably play an important role in the immediate future of adult education under University leadership.

Beginning July 1, 1946, the Extension Division, in cooperation with the Institute for Research in Social Science, will have the part-time services of a Director of Research Interpretation. It is a significant fact that the results of research must be translated in simple terms, clearly interpreted, and channeled through the existing media and agencies of adult education in order to render its greatest service to society and civilization. This should be one of the principal objectives not only of the Extension Division but also of the University. It may well shape and determine the future of University Extension and its relationship to the people of North Carolina.

I
HISTORICAL BACKGROUND

HISTORICAL BACKGROUND

C. E. MC INTOSH[*]

Throughout its existence, the University of North Carolina has sought to link its activities with those of the State. During the early years it was, of course, a small struggling institution, with little more income than was demanded by its work on the campus; for this reason, it had to confine its services to the public to such acts as writing letters in answer to specific inquiries, sending members of the faculty to address school commencements and similar gatherings, and making occasional surveys of the State's resources. Roughly, this type of unorganized contact with the people continued up to the outbreak of the Civil War.

When, in 1875, the University reopened its doors, it sensed keenly the need for a vastly expanded system of public schools, and both President Battle and his faculty would gladly have furnished the leadership required had they been free to do so. At that time, however, the operating budget was under even more stringent limitations than during the later years of the previous era; consequently, the University had to resort to a plan of doing vicariously the work which it could not do directly, that is, it had to inculcate its ideals in the minds of students and trust them to carry the message to the people.

Perhaps no other University decision ever achieved greater results; for in less than a decade a group of vigorous young educational evangelists went forth from the campus, each fired with consuming zeal for better public schools. The accomplishments of four of these in particular may be mentioned by way of illustration.

---

[*] Mr. C. E. McIntosh is Acting Head of the Bureau of High School Relations of the University Extension Division. He was Executive Secretary of the School of Education from 1927 to 1933.

In the 1880's, the State Department of Public Instruction employed Charles D. McIver and Edwin A. Alderman, recent University graduates, to hold a series of teachers' institutes in all parts of North Carolina. Both entered enthusiastically upon their new tasks, their plan of procedure being to hold professional meetings with teachers and prospective teachers for the first four days of the week, and on the last day of the week to invite the public to a general educational rally. Wherever they went they stimulated the average man and woman to a belief in better schools, and before the close of their campaign the legislature had been persuaded to establish at Greensboro the State Normal and Industrial College, now the Woman's College of the University of North Carolina. The chief purpose of this institution was to train teachers for public school work. McIver became its first president and for a time Alderman was a member of its faculty. Their slogan was, "The teacher is the seed-corn of civilization, and none but the best is good enough to use." Their first graduates became teachers in 1893, each carrying into her community the doctrine that only through greater enlightenment could North Carolina hope to solve its weighty problems and take its rightful position in the sisterhood of states.

In 1900, Charles B. Aycock, of the same University generation, was elected Governor. He came to office with but one avowed purpose, to place a good public school within reach of every boy and girl in the State. During the four years of his administration, and indeed up to the time of his death in 1912, he devoted his energies and his great eloquence to the uplift of the common man, his most famous phrase being "North Carolina is too poor not to educate her children." As he left the Governor's chair, he made the proud boast that for each day since his inauguration his State had built a public schoolhouse.

In 1903, when the State Superintendent of Public Instruction died, Aycock appointed his college mate, James Y. Joyner, to fill the unexpired term. The new appointee, like McIver, Alderman, and Aycock, eagerly grasped his opportunity, his major thesis being that since the education of its children is so important to each community, the city, village, or school district ought to vote local taxes for extended school terms and better prepared teachers. His argument prevailed, and for the next fifteen years it was news when a local school-tax election failed of approval by the voters. Joyner remained as superintendent until 1919, by which time North Carolina was a virtual network of local tax districts with a fifty per cent longer average school term than prevailed a decade earlier. Since he relinquished active leadership and retired to private life, he has continued to be a staunch and able advocate of general popular enlightenment.

These four alumni are but representative of many others who undertook to carry the University ideal to citizens dwelling at a distance. The combined labors of all are a testimony to the University's desire to serve, although it could not itself enter more fully into the work which it so heartily approved.

The Beginnings of University Extension

By 1907 the University was able to extend its services to the public in a more direct manner. The library under the direction of Dr. Louis R. Wilson moved that year into a large, well planned library building. Wilson classified and arranged everything according to modern standards, and found that he could, if he but had the proper channel for distribution, make a great amount of reading matter available to the public. In his report to the President, he said that books and pamphlets are of small value, so long as they remain on library shelves, that the University ought to have some means of lending these books and pamphlets to schools, clubs, and individuals, so that they might be of actual service. This belief of the librarian gave initial impetus to what is now called University Extension.

N. W. Walker had come to the University in 1905, as professor of secondary education. When, in 1907, the legislature established a fund for the aid of secondary instruction, Walker became State Inspector of High Schools. In traveling about the State, he at once saw the need for better library facilities. Since no legal provision had been made for adequate school libraries, he suggested to the superintendents and principals that they borrow books from the University. This plan proved a godsend, for it brought University and communities closer together and enabled each to appreciate the problems of the other. University Extension began to function through the cooperation of the librarian, the State Inspector of High Schools, and school officials.

In the fall of 1912, the two literary societies of the University, the Dialectic and the Philanthropic, sought to stimulate in high schools the same type of debating program which they had carried on for a century. They proposed to select a query, to prepare and publish a bulletin containing arguments both pro and con, and to distribute this bulletin to any high school which would agree to carry into effect the general plan of operation. The announcement that such a discussion program would be offered met with instant and widespread approval, and the societies were encouraged to provide a joint committee of students to put the plans into execution. Librarian Wilson and State School Inspector Walker became faculty advisers to the student committee, and helped steer the new enterprise through its first tentative venture. To their wisdom is due in large measure the success immediately attained. The High School Debating Union, as it was called, enrolled the first year ninety high schools scattered throughout North Carolina. The outcome of the first annual contest was highly encouraging. Newspapers spoke glowingly of the service which the Debating Union had rendered to the people. The organization grew rapidly until, by 1917, three hundred and thirty-two high schools had enrolled and the combined audiences reached into the thousands. High school debating at once found its place in University Extension.

The Faculty Committee

In the fall of 1911, President Francis P. Venable appointed a faculty committee to study the whole question of how the University might more adequately serve the State's citizens. The chairman of this committee was Dr. Edwin Mims, and his associate members were E. K. Graham, M. H. Stacy, A. H. Patterson, and N. W. Walker. During the year Dr. Mims resigned from the faculty and accepted a position at his alma mater, Vanderbilt University. His place as chairman was taken by Dr. Louis R. Wilson who was vitally concerned with providing better services to the people. His report to the President, December 1912, summarizes what the committee did during the year of study:

1. Investigated the types of work usually considered as university extension
2. Held a series of lectures on literary topics at Winston-Salem
3. Planned for further lectures in cooperation with other colleges in the State, and with the State Literary and Historical Commission
4. Provided for the lending of materials from the University Library
5. Agreed upon plans for enlarging extension work in the future

The committee having been given an allotment of six hundred dollars from the University's printing fund, issued two bulletins, one entitled "A Professional Library for Teachers in Secondary Schools," and the other "Addresses on Education for Use in Declamation, Essay-Writing, and Reading." Two thousand copies of the former and four thousand copies of the latter were quickly distributed on order. More than eight hundred copies of the latter were requested after the issue had been exhausted. The committee felt, therefore, that there was a genuine demand for the type of service it proposed. With the survey already made, there was needed only a functioning organization.

The Bureau of Extension

Such an organization was established in 1913. It was called the Bureau of Extension, and consisted of a faculty committee headed by the University Librarian, Dr. Louis R. Wilson. It received the full support of Acting-President E. K. Graham, who had been a member of the faculty committee from 1911 to 1913, and through him, when he became President in 1914, was given a place of first importance in the work of the University. His aid was particularly valuable in providing funds for the establishment of the Department of Rural Social-Economics (1914), under Professor E. C. Branson, and for the publication of *The University of North Carolina News Letter* and *The North Carolina Club Yearbook* which were edited by Professor Branson and were widely distributed throughout the State. The following list of services, together with the names of those responsible for their direction, indicates the manner in which the Bureau, in the first half decade of its existence, attempted to coordinate and expand the extension activities of the University:

1. General Information—Director Wilson
2. Social and Economic Surveys—Prof. E. C. Branson
3. Public Discussion and Debate—Asst. Director Rankin

4. Correspondence Instruction—Prof. L. A. Williams
5. Lectures—Asst. Director Rankin
6. Municipal Reference—Profs. Raper and Hamilton
7. Educational Information—Profs. Noble, Walker, Williams, and Chase
8. Good Roads Institute*—Joseph Hyde Pratt
9. Medical Instruction**—Asst. Director Rankin
10. Improvement of School Grounds—Prof. W. C. Coker

Under this division of labor, the Bureau carried on its work. It had no limited field of endeavor nor did it have a pet program. Its job was to work with and through departments and agencies already established, and to use experts already available, rather than to employ personnel of its own. By so doing, it naturally drew to itself many clubs, associations, and groups, some of which had problems of a more or less lasting character, and some of which needed temporary help until they could take over their activities independently. It is, therefore, entirely beyond the scope of this sketch to go into detail concerning the various types of work performed or to evaluate any particular undertaking.

The University had reached the people. The people sought an ever-closer relationship with their University.

By 1920, the Bureau had become too important to be operated on a voluntary basis. The numerous departments and agencies concerned were anxious to maintain their relationships with the Bureau, but they could no longer do the enormous amount of work required. It became necessary, therefore, to broaden the organization, to select a full-time director, and to give him a special staff. This was done, when in 1920 the Bureau of Extension became the University Extension Division, and Chester D. Snell was appointed Director.

---

* In cooperation with the State Department of Highway Engineering
** In cooperation with the State Board of Health

The University Extension Division

Under President H. W. Chase, several changes were made in University organization. Among them was the expansion of the University Extension Division.

In his first report as director of the Division (December, 1921) Mr. Snell states that the Division had been sub-divided into thirteen bureaus, each under the supervision of a faculty member or a member of the staff. These bureaus continued all of the work which had been found of special value and added new activities. A list of bureaus indicates the type of work carried on:

- High School Debating and Athletics
- Educational Information and Assistance
- Public Discussion (Library Extension Service)
- Community Drama
- Economic and Social Surveys
- Community Music
- Design and Improvement of School Grounds
- Municipal Information and Research
- Community Organization
- Commercial and Industrial Relations
- Correspondence and Class Instruction
- Extension Lectures
- Short Courses and Institutes

These thirteen bureaus at once set about their tasks, and each met with flattering public response. A year later the director reported that the Division had prepared and circulated in the State nearly one million copies of pamphlets and bulletins, each dealing with some specific public interest. In addition to previous activities there had been added: a high school essay contest on "How Good Roads Are Developing in My Community," a high school typewriting contest, an inspection service among schools of twelve nearby counties, a reading circle course for the teachers of a large city school unit, work with 167 women's clubs with a membership of nearly 3,000, aid to 145 units of the Parent-Teacher Association, community pageants in a half-dozen local settings, aid to twelve school systems in installing supervisors of music, fifteen lectures to chambers of commerce, factory councils, insurance institutes, and Kiwanis and Rotary clubs, etc. These, together with a greatly expanded program of correspondence and class instruction and a number of new short courses and institutes relating to various topics, comprised the work of the first biennium under the reorganization.

In 1923 there were 901 students enrolled in extension classes and 609 in correspondence courses, or a total off-campus enrollment of 1510 students. By 1924 the number of such students had risen to 2,638, approximately the same as the number of resident students. In 1925 there were 2,823 individual off-campus students registered for 3,969 courses. This single type of extension growth shows how greatly the people of the State had come to depend upon the University for educational services.

In 1926, Director Snell accepted a similar position at the University of Wisconsin. He was succeeded by Russell M. Grumman, who served as Acting Director until he was named Director in September 1928.

At the outset of his administration, President Frank P. Graham publicly expressed his interest in University Extension. He has continuously emphasized its importance in the life of the University and of the State. It is his conception that the University of North Carolina is and should remain "The University of the People," also, that University Extension is one of the chief means through which this ideal may be fully achieved. In his inaugural address (1931) he said:

"It is the function of the state university not only to find its bits of truth and teach the truth gathered from scholars everywhere, but to carry the truth to the people that they may take it into their lives and help to make it prevail in the world of affairs. It is the ideal of the University Extension Division to make the resources of the universities, the discoveries of science, and the findings of the social scientists available for the people of the commonwealth. The members of the general faculty, the special library, special lectures, courses in class and by correspondence, bureaus, institutes, inter-scholastic activities involving athletics, debates, Latin, plays and playwriting, and, in an independent and far-reaching way, the general library and the Library School, all serve to carry or send the University to the people.

"The state university comes from the people and should go out to the people. The intellectual life of the university should be quickened by contact and interchange with the people. They have a common destiny in the adventure of building a nobler commonwealth. The state university cannot, as the university of the people, be an institution of a class, whether based on blood, money, or intellectual background. The state university can never lose the common touch without treason to its own nature and without drying up the springs from which flows the living waters of its own life.

"Now is the time in the midst of depression, unemployment, and educational defeatism for the Extension Division and the public schools to envisage and lay out the plans for a future all-inclusive educational program in the communities for the continuous education of all of the people as a way to use wisely the advancing leisure, to substitute cultural content for merely mechanical contacts, natural creative play for artificial and empty excitement, and to lay the intellectual groundwork for a more general and intelligent understanding of and participation in the affairs of the world and its opportunities for a larger mastery of human destiny."

THE DIRECTORATE OF EXTENSION

One of the first acts of the President, following the consolidation in 1933 of the University of North Carolina, State College of Agriculture and Engineering, and The North Carolina College for Women, was the appointment of a Directorate of Extension. The Director of the University Extension Division at Chapel Hill was named chairman, who with the Directors of Extension at each of the other instituitons compose the Directorate.

It formulates major policies and plans for University Extension of the consolidated University. Thus, duplication of effort is avoided and the resources of the three institutions are made available to the people of the State.

II
TEACHING SERVICES

TEACHING SERVICES

One of the major functions of the modern state university is continuing or adult education. University administrators are cognizant of the fact that the responsibility of the university for the educational life of the people of the state is not met on graduation day. Hence many opportunities are being developed so that adults may continue their education.

This obligation to all the people of the State has determined the pattern of extension activity. The development of extension teaching services has been an attempt to meet the educational needs of people off-campus. Originally planned in cooperation with the public school system and its own program of "In-service Teacher Training" such service has long since been expanded to meet requests from varied business and civic groups.

Extension teaching is never a static procedure. No catalog of courses offered can be printed for a year's program. Such services are built entirely upon requests, and vary not only from year to year, but from town to town, month by month.

A complete discussion of all teaching services rendered to the citizens of North Carolina would be prohibitively long, but a review of the work as carried on in five specific fields will serve to show the possibilities.

Extension Class Instruction

The story of extension teaching in North Carolina is as thrilling as that of the work of the circuit rider of by-gone days. Meeting a teaching schedule in the remote corners of the State has challenged not only the stamina of the instructor but the ingenuity of the nearest garage mechanic, who must keep the over-used Ford on schedule.

Extension classes, taught by members of the University faculty, have been held in practically every section of the State.

Starting in 1920-1921 before the hard-surfaced road made an easy path to distant towns, these instructors braved the red mud of back roads to carry knowledge to those who requested it.

In the early days most of the classes were for teachers who were raising their certificates while still on the job. Education, History, Music, Geography, English, Psychology, and Physical Education were the most popular courses. At each center two courses, or four-half-courses, were offered during the academic year. Extension courses carry the equivalent in content and time requirements as courses given in residence; therefore the same amount of credit is offered. The amount of credit earned by such instruction is, however, limited to thirteen and one-half courses.

At first classes were taught by resident faculty members only, who rushed to a nearby town for evening classes, or who spent their weekends meeting students in more distant parts of the State. Such a plan, controlled by the time involved as well as by the mileage, naturally limited the radius of service. As requests for classes increased it became necessary to employ full-time extension instructors. These full-time instructors organized their territory into circuits, going from town to town and returning to each group once a week. In order that these off-campus centers might have similar advantages as those offered at the University each instructor carried with him a traveling library, slides, maps, film strips, records, art reproductions, scientific apparatus and such other teaching aids as might be appropriate to a given situation. Loaded with such supplies, and stopping regularly at the same hotels, it is no wonder these men and women became known as "peddlers of education."

From 1926 to 1930 eight such full-time instructors were employed, who made their headquarters in the section of the State where their classes were to be held. Instructors who were holding classes for public school personnel were thus able to devote much time in visitation and supervision, thereby rendering many additional professional services to the community. Out of this close working arrangement grew the present plan of "In-service Teacher Education." Such teaching service carried direct to the community has enabled many teachers and school administrators to raise their professional standards and helped raise the standard of education in the State.

Extension teaching services were created as a result of the requirements placed upon teachers to raise and renew their teaching certificates, but the service was not long limited to educators. Upon request, classes have been organized for social workers, public welfare officials, business men, manufacturers, salesmen, doctors, dentists, accountants, housewives, club women, churchmen and others. Some of the courses have carried regular University credit toward a degree, but many of them have been attended purely for reasons of personal improvement and cultural background. The subjects taught have been as varied as the groups making the requests, but always the class has contributed to the educational need of an adult group.

A woman's club in a remote mountain village requested a course in Art Appreciation. The instructor, a member of the Art Department, made a weekly trip to meet the class. On one occasion, when the roads were icy, her timing was thrown off schedule and she found it necessary to seek lodging in an isolated farm house. The warmth of the welcome was gratifying, but space and heat were limited and she found herself "bedded down for the night" with two small children on a pallet in front of the open fire. Due to improved roads and more reliable cars, such experiences are now history, but they serve to show the pioneering spirit that made possible the present day network of extension classes throughout the State.

Correspondence Instruction

Correspondence Instruction was one of the initial activities of the Extension Division. As early as 1913 non-credit courses were offered by means of the home study method of instruction. Since then the idea of obtaining knowledge by this means has expanded, until now it is possible to earn one year of academic credit (nine courses) toward an undergraduate degree. Courses are offered by practically every department of the University with the exception of the natural sciences.

Only minimum registration and course fees are charged. In conformity with the practice at other state colleges and universities, correspondence instruction is considered a part of the University's service to the State, therefore, it is administered on virtually a cost basis although out-of-state students are charged slightly higher fees.

Correspondence instruction is designed to provide individual instruction. In order to achieve this objective, special techniques of teaching and a plan of supervision have been developed. University standards have been maintained and safeguarded. The courses are arranged on the basis of from 15 to 30 lessons, each of which is equivalent to two class periods at the University. In addition to the use of textbooks, required in most courses, supplementary reading material is made available to correspondence students through the Extension Library Service.

A total of one hundred and fifty correspondence courses are now offered. Since 1920, more than twenty-three thousand adult students have been enrolled. These students are located in every county in North Carolina, in thirty other states and in a few foreign countries. They represent over fifty vocations. Many of them are former college students who for economic, or other reasons, have had to suspend their study in residence. Some are high school graduates starting their college study while earning money for the stay in Chapel Hill. Others are handicapped physically and find correspondence study their only means of continuing their education. Still others are adults in pursuit of intellectual, cultural or vocational courses which will raise their professional rating.

Letters from students frequently explain their reasons for enrolling and tell of successes they have achieved because of their study. A member of the New York Giants baseball team wrote that he was studying diligently in order to complete the course he was taking for degree credit before time to join the other players in their annual practice in Florida. A nurse serving as a missionary in India explained she hoped that by taking a certain course she would receive help in developing a village health program. A student from Utah who was registered for a course in playwriting, had one of his plays published in Kozlenko's "One Hundred One Act Plays"; and a club woman who was a student in a short story course, won the Joseph P. Caldwell award for her story "November Night."

Not all attain such success but the thrill of accomplishment is shared by all who meet a need. This is evident in the following taken from a recent letter: "I'm sure glad to finish this course. It was hard sometimes to concentrate in the hut with thirty Sea Bees and a radio."

A group study plan of correspondence instruction has been developed in a few communities. Under the direction of a qualified teacher or study supervisor the plan offers students some of the advantages of class instruction and discussion. Many high school graduates unable to attend college have made use of this plan, as have adult education teachers, parents, and other civic groups.

A faculty committee has made a careful study of supervised correspondence study for high school students. Due to the number of small high schools in the State which are understaffed it is apparent that many students are handicapped by the limited number of courses offered. Should the University offer correspondence courses in secondary school subjects, it would be able to increase greatly its service to the State.

During the war, correspondence courses were offered to the men and women in the armed forces. That story will be found in the chapter entitled "University Extension in Wartime."

These services are rendered by the Bureau of Correspondence Instruction. Beginning with the services of a faculty member who gave part time supervision without extra pay, and a part time secretary who handled the clerical work and routine matters, it has grown to a full-sized department. At present the staff consists of a Bureau Head, an assistant, a supervisor of instruction and three full-time clerical workers, with part-time people coming in to help during rush seasons. The preparation of courses and the correction of papers requires the part-time services of about 150 faculty members.

Miss Mary Louisa Cobb has served as Head of the Bureau of Correspondence Instruction since 1921. Under her expert guidance and direction the service has been conducted in accordance with the best standards and procedures of teaching by correspondence.

Special Aspects of Extra-Mural In-service Teacher Education

ROY W. MORRISON[*]

During the period 1921 to about 1932 the University of North Carolina engaged in a very extensive program of in-service teacher education through extension courses that were

---

[*] Director, Bureau of Educational Research and Service; Chairman, Committee on Off-Campus Work in Education.

offered in centers scattered rather haphazardly over the State. The location of centers was determined largely by demand and was limited only by personnel, difficulties of transportation, and agreements with other institutions, a number of which also engaged extensively in such activities.

The courses were limited by University policy to those set up for regular residence work. Personnel consisted partially of regular staff members of various departments, who conducted extension courses in addition to their other departmental duties and who were paid supplementary fees for the work. Additional staff members were employed by departments at the request of the Extension Division and their salaries were paid by the Division in accordance with the regular University schedule. Administratively all extension work was under the Extension Division, but the supervision of the instructional assignments and standards was nominally under departmental control. No recognized policies obtained in the sequence of courses, the assignment of personnel, or the instructional procedures in any particular center. The acceptance of students and the earning of credit was controlled only by certification policies of the State Department of Public Instruction in the case of state employed teachers and principals, and by University regulations in the case of students regularly registered in the University for degrees. Some attempts were made by staff members cooperatively to maintain standards of instruction and to adapt these to the opportunities and limitations of field study. A large part of the financial support was earned income from tuition fees. Most of the work was done on an undergraduate level. It was carried on without relation to local school administration, local supervision, or locally important purposes and problems, except as the individual instructor might work these out. Most of the students were working according to plans for securing higher teaching certificates, rather than according to plans for securing a college degree. Provisions had, however, been made for graduate students to earn approximately twenty per cent of the credits toward a Master's degree under instructors who were members of the graduate faculty of the University.

Around 1935 the demands of teachers for extension courses in which they could earn credits toward higher teaching certification were definitely diminishing. (The proportion of all North Carolina's white teachers holding A certificates, representing the equivalent of four years college training, had reached approximately 93% by 1941). At the time that some of the newer trends in in-service education and in supervision became clear, the number of teachers and principals who were working toward graduate degrees was increasing, and local professional groups were becoming more active in projects of local significance. During this period the old type of extension classes declined greatly in enrollment, and many other institutions in the State abandoned their extension class programs.

Between 1932 and 1937 several classes were organized in which the membership was limited to principals, superintendents, and to teachers who were recommended by administrators as outstanding in potential leadership. The courses of study were built around problems and projects of local significance. In four cases tuition fees were paid in part by the county or city Board of Education. Credits earned were almost wholly graduate credits. Approximately three hundred different students were enrolled in such classes. Local administrative personnel and projects were made a definite part of the program.

In three cases these centers became cooperative, non-credit projects. A fee approximating the average income received by the University from tuition fees in a center was paid to the University by the Board of Education. The instructor became an adviser to the local administration, to local planning councils of teachers and principals, and to committees of teachers engaged in professional study and in projects in curriculum or school program improvement. One day a week throughout the school year was spent in visitation and in conferences. There still was no official institutional recognition of the possibilities of this type of in-service teacher education as an integrated part of a total teacher education program.

During 1939, as a part of the planning undertaken by the University in its cooperation with the Commission on Teacher Education, a review was made of the program of in-service education of teachers. The need was recognized for organization, policies, and procedures which would make this a part of a more progressive, more cohesive total program of teacher education. It was recognized: (a) that the provision of a graduate teaching certificate based on a graduate degree in North Carolina would create a great demand for field training on the graduate level; (b) that the University would profit greatly from wider, more intimate, more functional relationships with the schools of the State; (c) that summer school students would do much more valuable work if definite needs and problems significant in the teacher's local teaching situation and in her own professional growth were recognized in advance of her registration in the courses of her program of graduate sutdy; (d) that the resources of the University should be made available to groups of teachers, principals, and superintendents who, independently or as a part of the program of professional organizations or that of the State Department of Public Instruction, might be undertaking projects in the improvement of education locally; and (e) that certain school systems in the State might serve as valuable laboratories in graduate and undergraduate teacher education as well as in the after-graduation guidance of teachers. It was recognized that the development of such a program would soon require the coordination of the interests, resources, and activities of all the various institutions in the State which were engaged in teacher education.

Since the development of such a program would involve a considerable period of study and experimentation, the following possibilities were seen as immediately available for experimentation:

1. A program of graduate study in Saturday classes for principals and teachers at Greensboro and Chapel Hill. This was to be worked out by using the regular faculty, making it a part of the regular University program and developing it along lines found to be most useful to teachers and principals in terms of their own purposes and problems. This has been in operation for four years. During 1940-41 limitations were placed on the amount which this type of study should represent in a student's total program of graduate work and on the amount which a student might do in any one school year. The amount was limited to one-half of a student's total program and to ten quarter hours in any one school year. A careful study of the experience is now being made, with a view to making any desirable changes in the program.

2. A further development of extension classes on a graduate level. This was to be undertaken so far as demand and personnel permitted. These were to be primarily laboratory courses which were to be utilized not only by the individual student for his or her purposes and problems, but by the school system for the study of locally significant problems and for the development of curriculum materials and plans for local professional projects. Two notable examples of this were worked out: (a) in Gastonia by Dr. W. E. Rosenstengel in curriculum evaluation and in planning for a period of curriculum revision; (b) in Columbus County by Dr. Rosenstengel and by Dr. John Ludington of State College in curriculum study with special emphasis on Industrial Arts. One difficulty has proved to be

that the program of study is financed by the fees of individual students and hence the school system has no special stake in the experiment. In these two cases this was off-set by the provision by the Board of Education, and by the joint financing of a special series of conferences for all the teachers and principals of the system.

3. The development of a number of non-credit extension centers. Two of these have been under way for some time, in Cleveland County and in Stanly County. The latter includes also the city system of Albemarle. One was carried on for a year in Rutherford County, but was discontinued because no one from the faculty could be released by the University to carry it on. An additional center is planned for in Gastonia, supplemented by a credit study center, which is planned primarily for the teachers and principals of Gaston County. The cost in each case is carried by the school system.

In each of these centers, one day a week is spent by a faculty member in visiting schools and classrooms with the superintendent of schools. These visits represent conference periods with teachers and principals spent in discussing problems and projects included in the program. The afternoon and early evening are spent in conference with committees of teachers or principals engaged in study or production. In each case the program is planned and directed by a committee of teachers and principals with the superintendent and instructor acting as consultants. Time and financial limitations have prevented full utilization of the University's resources in these centers. To a limited extent, experiences in these centers have been utilized in summer school programs, especially in the workshops of 1940-41.

4. A program of close cooperation with and service to state and local teacher organizations. There are two objectives in this program: First, to serve worthy undertakings which repre-

sent teacher growth and the improvement of education; and second to utilize the outcomes of such undertakings in the program of teacher education. During a four year period 1938-42 the major emphasis of the North Carolina Education Association was the stimulation of programs of professional study, experimentation and development in local professional groups. Handbooks for the stimulation and guidance of such projects were developed by a State Planning Committee.

During three of these years 1939-42 the writer was chairman of the State Planning Committee, and, with other members of the faculty, cooperated very actively in promoting and directing this program both in regional meetings and in local units of the Association. In addition, the campus facilities were extensively used for cooperative planning conferences by the Association and by its departments, notably the Department of Classroom Teachers. Further cooperation in preparing bulletins has been sought by this and other departments, most recently by the Elementary Principals.

One direct outcome of this cooperation was the workshop program of 1940 and 1941. These workshops were sponsored jointly by the Association and the University. Most of the participants and many teachers and principals who began their graduate study during this period had been very active in the Association's state and local activities. In one case, in the Summer School of 1940, twenty-seven teachers and principals were enrolled from one county which had been very active and in which one of the cooperative centers, described in section 3 above, was located.

5. A program of systematic cooperation, assistance and guidance for groups of teachers and for local school administrators. This program as it develops is intended to supplement and to extend the four developments listed above. It is planned that the Bureau of Educational Research and Service shall be the

coordinating and distributive agency for this phase of field activity. In the past this Bureau has been chiefly a test sales and service agency. The research and broader service aspects were envisioned from its beginnings under Dr. M. R. Trabue. These were more specifically provided for during the departmental administration of Dr. Harl R. Douglass, in 1939. Lack of funds and limitation of personnel have prevented extensive development.

The Bureau is now engaged in all of the developments described above. As rapidly as funds can be secured and the resources of the Department and of the whole University can be utilized, the following forms of service will be developed:

a. Cooperative surveys of schools and school systems.
b. A further development of cooperation in work conferences and institutes.
c. Bulletins of information and suggestion for use by school groups.
d. Bulletins reporting valuable experiments and development in the field.
e. Bibliographies for use by study groups and in building professional libraries.
f. Correspondence service on questions and problems from the field.

In all of this, besides problems of financing, organization, direction and evaluation, two problems are of vital significance. While some progress has been made with each of them, much more careful study and careful planning and execution remains to be done. The first problem is coordination with the purposes and activities of the State Department of Public Instruction. The relations between the University and the State Department have always been close. During recent years valuable progress has been made in three projects: the development of new teaching and administrative certificates on a graduate level;

the development of a statewide study of teacher education, one phase of which is "a study of professional growth and study by teachers in service"; and in planning the transition from an eleven to a twelve year curriculum for the schools of the State. The second is coordination of the field activities of the institutions of the State that are engaged in teacher education, especially the state supported institutions. The basis for such a co-ordinated program is being laid in the on-campus program, but the problem of coordination of field activities remains to be attacked.

In 1944-45 a committee from the Department of Education was appointed to study the whole program of off-campus teacher education. This Committee recommended to the Department and to the Extension Division certain policies. The purposes of these recommendations were: (1) to coordinate the off-campus and the on-campus work of the Department as to personnel, courses, and non-instructional services; (2) to maintain high standards of graduate instruction and to provide more careful guidance for beginning graduate students; (3) to carry on a more careful selection of service centers; (4) to provide for better collaboration between the University and other agencies, particularly the local administrator and local teachers associations in planning and carrying out the program of service in the several centers selected each year.

During this period increasing numbers of requests for extension classes, for local workshops, for consultant service, and for non-credit study-direction have come from administrators and from teacher groups who want assistance in professional programs locally planned and administered. In some instances classes serve as planning and work centers for activities which involve the whole personnel of a county or city school system. In one instance, 1945-46 is the third year of an experiment in cooperative supervision. In another, a city and county system are using a non-credit study center to begin a cooperative evaluation of the school program. In still another, a summer workshop is being planned to further a program of curriculum study already begun on a non-credit study basis.

Post-Graduate Medical and Dental Courses

Two large professional groups which have taken advantage of the teaching services offered by the Extension Division have been the doctors and the dentists. The first course for doctors was held in 1916. Since then post-graduate medical courses have been considered a regular extension activity, even though there have been interruptions in the schedules due to economic and war conditions. The story of that first class is ably told by Dr. Louis R. Wilson in Bulletin No. 7 of the U. S. Department of the Interior.

"Conservation of Public Health has received steadily increasing consideration throughout North Carolina from many individuals, organizations, and public institutions during the past decade. Among these has been the university, whose participation in the campaign for increased physical welfare has been expressed through the members of its medical faculty. In order to further emphasize the importance of this matter and render a more extensive service than was practical through the first two-year medical courses given by its medical department and through the occasional addresses delivered by members of the medical faculty, the university, at the suggestion of Secretary W. S. Rankin, of the State board of health, in the summer of 1916 instituted post-graduate courses in medicine for the benefit of practicing physicians. This work, which proved very successful, was carried on jointly by the university and the State board of health.

"Two courses, both in pediatrics, were conducted, one being for physicians in eastern Carolina, the other in western Carolina. One was for 16 weeks, the other for 12 weeks. They consisted of lectures and clinics under the direction of Dr. Lewis Webb Hill of Harvard University, and Dr. Jesse R. Gertsley, of Northwestern University, both acknowledged experts in their field.

"Under this plan the teacher went to the doctors practicing at home, instead of a few of the best of them going north to him, for several weeks of clinical work. Six towns in eastern North Carolina reasonably close together, with satisfactory train schedules, were selected, and a class of physicians (varying in number from 8 to 20) was formed in each town from the town and its surrounding country. The first lecture was given to the class in town A on Monday morning for one hour, and a two-hour clinic held that afternoon. On Tuesday the lecturer went to town B for the first lecture there; on Wednesday to town C; and so on through the six towns on the six days of the week, going back to town A on the following Monday for the second lecture; and so on for the second lecture and clinic at B, C, etc., and so on through the length of the course. In this way the lectures in town A were all delivered on Monday, those in town B on Tuesday, etc., and similarly for the western division.

"One hundred and eighty-five physicians took the courses, or above 90 in each division. The expenses of the course were paid by the physicians, the tuition charges being about $30 for each student. A small laboratory in the local hospital was maintained in connection with each clinic."

After this fine beginning World War I caused an interruption, but by 1922 classes were revived and continued with such success that the project attracted considerable attention beyond the boarders of the State. It became known as "The North Carolina Plan" and was adopted by other states. A second break in the annual schedule came with the depression. But again in 1936, at the request of the late Dr. W. H. Smith of Goldsboro, the idea was put into operation with renewed enthusiasm.

The plan followed was fundamentally that of the original class. The advent of the automobile made transportation much simpler and it was found that doctors would attend classes from a radius of fifty miles. Instead of having morning classes the dinner meeting was initiated. Keeping abreast of new teaching techniques, the instructor used films and slides to illustrate his lectures. The laboratory clinics, still considered essential, were held in the afternoon with the visiting lecturer in charge.

The responsibility for the organization of the class was placed upon the local or county medical society in cooperation with the Extension Division. The choice of subjects and lecturers was left largely to local committees of society members, but the Extension Division made all the arrangements and handled all financial matters.

Such courses have been held at Goldsboro, Raleigh, Charlotte, Greensboro, Greenville, Wilmington, Asheville and Durham. Attendance has varied from 55 to 250. Instructors have come from leading medical schools and centers in the United States, and represent the most forward thinking members of the profession.

The first post graduate course arranged for the dentists of the State was offered during the summer of 1928 and was the result of a cooperative effort on the part of the North Carolina Dental Society, Northwestern University Dental School, and the University of North Carolina Extension Division. The State was divided into five zones, with centers at Greenville, Raleigh, Greensboro, Winston-Salem, and Charlotte. The executive committee of the North Carolina Dental Society, working with a representative of the University Extension Division, planned the course, being guided in the selection of instructors and subjects to be included in the course by the replies to a questionaire which had been submitted to the members of the Society. The school from which the instructors were to be secured was decided upon by the executive committee, and local committees on organization and arrangement were appointed for the various centers. Newspaper stories, announcements at district and state meetings, and mimeographed material mailed to the Society's members were the methods employed to get the necessary information regarding the classes before the dentists.

Ten instructors were used, each one spending a week in the State giving a lecture, illustrated by the use of models and lantern slides, in each center.

The success of this first attempt warranted the continuation of the project. Each succeeding year dentists throughout the

State have had this opportunity to keep abreast of new developments in their profession.

Temporarily discontinued because of the war, these classes will, no doubt, be resumed at an early date.

Short Courses and Institutes

Teaching services through short courses and institutes annually serve more people than the regular University enrollment. These programs are the outgrowth of the educational needs of civic and professional organizations. Such groups submit their requests to the Extension Division which works out cooperative arrangements with the appropriate University department. The groups served vary from women's club leaders and Boy Scout executives to highly specialized scientific organizations. Likewise the amount of service rendered by the Extension Division varies with the length of course and the amount of leadership required. Not all such courses or institutes are held on the campus. They may be held at any place requested by the group to be served.

These short courses and institutes fall into the following three classifications, based upon the manner in which they originate and the amount of University assistance they receive: Those initiated by the University to fill a recognized need; those which are an outgrowth of year-round service to an organization; and, those planned by the University at the request of an organization to fill an immediate need.

INITIATED BY THE UNIVERSITY

Many short courses and institutes now held on the campus originated as a result of educational needs expressed by groups of citizens or as interpreted by University faculty members. Such courses of from three to six weeks duration are taught by college teachers, some of whom are chosen from the University faculty.

Many of these short, intensive courses carry college credit while others offer certificates of achievement or attendance. The courses are usually offered through the cooperation of the academic departments concerned and the Extension Division. The Extension Division carries on the necessary correspondence with the group desiring the course; arranges to select and employ approved instructors; clears with the Dean's office if credit is to be given; attends to publicity; orders textbooks and other supplies; makes arrangements for physical accommodations such as housing, feeding, laundry service, medical examinations, and extracurricular activities; and handles all the details of registration, including the collection of fees and paying of bills. The following incomplete list of short courses and institutes (with the names of the cooperating departments) is sufficient to illustrate the scope of the service:

Coaching School for Athletic Directors and Coaches
    Department of Physical Education and Athletics
Conference on the Conservation of Marriage and the Family
    Institute for Research in Social Science
Course in English for Latin Americans
    Inter-American Institute and Department of English
Courses for Teachers of the Physically Handicapped
    Department of Education
Courses in Nursing Education
    School of Public Health and Department of Education
Course in Photography
    Department of Physics
Creative Music Course
    Departments of Music and Education
English Institute
    English Extension and Department of English
French House
    Departments of Education and Romance Languages

High School Music Course
    Department of Music
High School Course in Dramatic Art
    Department of Dramatic Art
Intersession Summer Session for Teachers
    Department of Education
Institute for County Public Welfare Superintendents and Directors
    Division of Public Welfare and Social Work of the Graduate School
Institute of Public Health Dentistry
    School of Public Health and Department of Education
Institute on the Management of Children's Institutions
    Division of Public Welfare and Social Work of the Graduate School
Public Welfare Institute
    Division of Public Welfare and Social Work of the Graduate School
Portuguese House
    Department of Romance Languages
Public Health Nursing Course
    School of Public Health
Saturday Classes for Teachers
    Department of Education
Short Course for Sewerage Works Operators
    School of Public Health and Institute of Government
Social Work Institute for Public Welfare Case Workers
    Division of Public Welfare and Social Work of the Graduate School, Social Studies Institute, and the Institute for Research in Social Science
Southern Conference on Education
    All Departments participating
Workshop in Personnel Management
    School of Commerce

TEACHING SERVICES 45

RESULTING FROM YEAR-ROUND SERVICE TO AN ORGANIZATION

Over a period of years a number of State organizations have developed a working arrangement with the University whereby a department furnishes leadership on a more or less continuous basis. Frequently this is done by loaning a faculty member for a study or survey in a given field. In other cases the department representative may be asked to serve on a standing committee or may be appointed a member of the Executive Board and thus meet regularly with officials of the organization. Programs for the year are worked out and the organization thus kept informed of current developments through advice and consultation with educational leaders.

In such arrangements, the Extension Division becomes the liaison agency, bringing the department and the organization into working relationship. The Division also furnishes administrative assistance in carrying out the details of the programs planned. When the short course or institute is held, the Extension Division assumes responsibility for all local arrangements, including administrative and financial matters. These programs are purely for the professional, vocational, or self-improvement of the participating members. No academic credit is granted, but occasionally the University presents certificates of attendance to those who have met the announced requirements.

The following examples of this type of activity will serve to illustrate the range of interests represented:

Annual Bankers' Conference

> A representative of the School of Commerce is a regular contributor to "The Tar Heel Banker" and serves as a member of the program committee of the North Carolina Bankers' Association.

Insurance School

> A representative of the School of Commerce is a member

of the program committee of the North Carolina Association of Insurance Agents.

Annual Newspaper Institute
The Director of the Extension Division and representatives of the Department of Journalism and the University News Bureau are members of the program committee of the North Carolina Press Association.

Annual Boys' State
The Director of the Institute of Government and the Director of the Extension Division are members of the Boys' State Commission, North Carolina Department, The American Legion.

Annual Dramatic Festival
Members of the Playmakers staff, and the Director of the Extension Division are members of the Executive Committee of the Carolina Dramatic Association.

Annual Carolina Institute of International Relations
The Director of the Extension Division is chairman of the Institute Committee.

Annual Parent-Teacher Institute
The Director of the Extension Division is chairman of the Committee on College Cooperation and a member of the Board of Directors of the North Carolina Congress of Parents and Teachers.

ARRANGED BY THE UNIVERSITY AT THE REQUEST OF AN ORGANIZED GROUP

Some State and regional organizations turn to the University for assistance but do not expect continuous service throughout the year. Activities that develop on this basis are of shorter duration and not likely to become annual events. A department of the University usually provides professional leadership. The Extension Division supplies administrative assistance in carrying out the program and makes all local arrangements for the convenience of the visitors.

The variety and scope of these cooperative activities is indicated by the list of short courses and institutes given below, followed by their appropriate University sponsors—and the cooperating agencies.

    Boy Scout Jubilee, Department of Sociology—Boy Scouts of America, Region IV

    Health Education Conference, Department of Education—N. C. Education Association

    Linguistic Institute, Department of Romance Languages—American Council of Learned Societies

    Conference of the North Carolina Scholastic Press Association, Department of Journalism—State Department of Public Instruction

    Professional Relations Institute, Department of Education—N. C. Education Association

    Real Estate School, School of Commerce—N. C. Association of Real Estate Agents

    Regional Institute of the Family Service Association of America, Division of Public Welfare and Social Work of the Graduate School

    Rural Education Conference, Department of Education—Summer Session

    Safety Conference, Department of Education—N. C. Department of Highways and Institute of Government

    School Librarians' Conference, School of Library Science—Department of School Librarians, N. C. E. A.

    Science Teachers' Institute, Department of Education—Department of Science Teachers, N. C. E. A.

    State Bar Association Seminar, School of Law—N. C. Bar Association

    Summer School of Photography, Department of Physics—

N. C. Photographers Association

Symposium on Accounting and Taxation, School of Commerce—N. C. Association for C. P. A.'s

Study Tours

Prior to World War II, several educational tours were conducted by the Division for college students, public school teachers, and community leaders. A faculty committee on Foreign Study, under the leadership of Dr. William M. Dey, Head of the Department of Romance Languages, established standards regarding the awarding of academic credit for courses taken on foreign study tours. Summer tours were successfully carried out in both France and Germany during the period 1927 to 1931.

A transcontinental study tour was conducted in 1930. It was a motor-camping trip organized in two sections, one for those interested in natural sciences (botany, geology, and biology), the other for students of the social sciences (sociology, economics, and geography). There were 135 members of the tour, most of whom enrolled for the courses offered. Laboratory field work was a feature of each course. Similar study tours to the west coast, to Canada, and to Mexico were operated up to 1939.

The Department of Geology and Geography has been active in sponsoring summer field courses for a number of years. Such trips are administered, cooperatively, with the Extension Division.

III
LIBRARY EXTENSION SERVICE

LIBRARY EXTENSION SERVICE

AGATHA BOYD ADAMS*

The Library, under the leadership of Dr. Louis R. Wilson, can justly be termed the "Father of Extension" in the University of North Carolina. The ideals of service to the State, upon which the Extension Division is founded, were first realized through the activities of the Library.

In his annual report as Librarian in 1907, Dr. Wilson called attention to the amount of knowledge stored within the library walls, which could only be of value if shared with those who needed it, regardless of location. He proposed that a state-wide plan of distribution be made possible. While his proposal met with no opposition, neither did it secure action of a concrete nature. The chief supporter was a member of the Education faculty, Dr. N. W. Walker, who was also the State Inspector of High Schools. He saw in the idea an opportunity to aid schools throughout the State. At his suggestion principals and superintendents grasped at this chance to supplement the libraries in their communities, which were always inadequate, if indeed they existed at all.

Books, pamphlets, and other library materials were soon finding their way over the State. The people were becoming aware of the wealth of information which the University could provide. Requests grew in both number and range of subject.

By 1911 the value of the service was so evident and its possibilities for expansion so desirable that a faculty committee was appointed to study ways and means of future development. This committee, after submitting its report, functioned as the Bureau of Extension with Dr. Louis R. Wilson as its Director. For many years Dr. Wilson retained this position in conjunction

---

* Associate Head, Library Extension Department

with his library work and the library remained headquarters for the Bureau of Extension.

The service to schools has continued through the years and has been adjusted to fit changing needs. As state appropriations have been made for school libraries, individual schools have become more self sufficient and have depended less upon the University for additional books. However, there always has been and still is a continuous flow to schools of material of a specialized nature which could not be obtained through their limited budgets.

In 1915, President Edward Kidder Graham sent to the Extension Bureau a letter from a clubwoman in the State who had been assigned a paper on "Robert Browning," and he felt, not without justification, that she needed help. President Graham suggested that the Extension Bureau might well provide such program assistance to the study clubs of the State. From this suggestion, and Dr. Wilson's still earlier provision for the needs of high schools, originated two of the major functions of the present Library Extension Department: work with schools and work with clubs.

At this time, Miss Nellie Roberson, Secretary of the Extension Bureau, was put in charge of the Women's Club Section. With Mrs. T. W. Lingle, then president of the North Carolina Federation of Women's Clubs, she planned the publication of Study Outlines to be used as club programs, the forerunners of the series of widely known *Library Extension Publications* which the Library Extension Department still publishes. The first of these was *A Study of Latin America*, by Professor W. W. Pierson of the University faculty.

The early growth of this type of Library Extension service was due largely to Dr. Wilson, who understood what such a service could mean to a State meagerly supplied with libraries, and who encouraged its progress in every possible way, both as

Librarian and later as Director of the Extension Bureau. Its steady development was, however, the work of Miss Roberson, who has for thirty years been director of this service. In the beginning she was a one-woman department, selecting and packaging books and answering letters and planning programs. Later she became director of a staff of five or six people in a busy office. Under her direction the number of Study Outlines published each year has increased from one to the present six. The selection of subjects of vital interest, and of writers with a knowledge of books and a talent for this type of outline presentation, has maintained a high standard of quality in the series.

Most of the Study Outlines have been prepared by members of the University faculty or of the Library staff. Some of them have had such distinquished authors as Paul and Elizabeth Green, Howard Mumford Jones, Addison Hibbard, Dr. J. F. Royster, Dr. R. D. W. Connor, and many others now on the faculty. Two series of these outlines have been so consistently popular that a new one is published each year: *Other People's Lives*, a lively program on current biography, was originated by Miss Cornelia Spencer Love, of the Library staff, and is still written by her. The other, *Adventures in Reading*, which was originated by Mrs. J. F. Royster and continued by Professor Russell Potter, has flourished through many adventures in authorship, including Dr. and Mrs. R. P. Bond, Agatha Adams, and Professor and Mrs. Walter Spearman. Among recent titles have been *Music in America*, by Adeline McCall; *Contemporary Poetry*, by Lucile Kelling; *Gardens of the South*, by Elizabeth Lawrence and *Journey to Mexico*, by Agatha Adams.

These Study Outlines are used not only in North Carolina but by clubs and libraries all over the country. About two hundred libraries regularly subscribe to the Outlines and twenty-five or more states besides North Carolina regularly use the services of the Library Extension Department.

In addition to the services to the schools and clubs, the Library Extension Department maintains a separate collection of books of special interest to students and teachers, particularly those enrolled in correspondence courses and in extension classes. This collection also includes plays, debates, and materials for essays and term papers.

Students taking courses through correspondence depend upon the Library Extension Department for supplementary reading material. In view of the fact that the Bureau of Correspondence Instruction annually offers more than 150 courses, the task of supplying this type of material is considerable. The titles for this collection are carefully selected by the cooperative effort of the Head of the Bureau of Correspondence Instruction, the author of the course, and the Head of the Library Extension Department.

It is not necessary, however, for an individual to be a member of a group or a student in school to obtain these privileges. The services and facilities are available to any citizen interested in cultural reading. Any book in the University Library, not reserved for reference or class room use, may be lent by mail for a limited time. The collection of books in the Library Extension Department is a functional one, neither large nor static. It is constantly revised, with approximately three hundred volumes withdrawn and the same number added each year. It consists of the books in club programs still actively in use, with a basic collection of older books. There is no need for a larger collection, since the Extension Library, in filling requests from out in the State, has the privilege of using the entire Library. The Extension collection is further supplemented by the Bull's Head Bookshop, which since 1937 has been housed in the same room and managed in cooperation with the Extension Library. The books in the shop may be either rented, for a small fee, or bought, and they also may be sent out of town through the Extension Department. Under the direction of Mrs. Charles Valentine, the Bull's Head Bookshop has become an important adjunct to the life of the University and the Library.

Perhaps the greatly-to-be-desired increase of libraries in the State and the expansion of bookmobile routes may at some future time render this type of loan service to readers unnecessary, but that millennium is still a long way off. Until it comes, the Library Extension Department will continue to furnish club programs, material for school debates and term papers, to assist correspondence students and to make books available to any one in the State who will write and ask for them.

IV
SCHOOL AND COMMUNITY ACTIVITIES

SCHOOL AND COMMUNITY ACTIVITIES

Generally speaking, most of the activities which are carried on by the Extension Division may be termed educational. Both individual and group learning results from all the subjects explained in this section. Yet, because they do not require prescribed textbooks and the usual classroom routine, they are discussed separately.

Recognizing the fact that all the departments of the University possess information and materials that could be utilized by the citizens of the State, the Extension Division endeavors to make known to the public the wealth of information and help that is available. As a result many regular services have been developed. As new requests are received the Director of Extension makes it his business to work out with the departments involved a satisfactory solution so that special services may be rendered to individuals and groups of persons concerned. More often, a department or interested faculty member initiates an idea for a new extension service to either the schools or community organizations.

Art

In an effort to create interest in and to promote art education in the schools of the State, the University cooperates with the North Carolina State Federation of Women's Clubs in sponsoring an annual school art exhibition.

The details of the plan were worked out in 1937, and the following year the first exhibition was presented. The Art Department and the Extension Division of the Woman's College at Greensboro share the responsibility of conducting the exhibition with the Art Department and the Extension Division at Chapel Hill.

Originally there were five divisions in the exhibition, namely, elementary schools, junior high schools, senior high schools, junior colleges, and senior colleges. The exhibition was shown in two parts. The first part made up of the elementary and high school divisions was shown at the Woman's College, and the second part composed of the college division was shown at the University. After a week's showing, the exhibits were exchanged so that the complete exhibition was displayed annually at each sponsoring institution.

The work of the elementary schools and junior high schools was shown as school units, while that of senior high schools and the colleges was exhibited as the work of individuals. Awards were given in various classifications, to the first and second place winners. Honorable mention was also made at the discretion of the judge. Exhibitors were charged a small entry fee to help pay the cost of the project. Entries were made in many classifications. The 1945 Extension Bulletin announcing the eighth annual exhibition lists the following: Illustration; Posters; Modeling and Carving; Watercolor Painting, Tempera, Showcard; Prints; Costume Design; Portraits; Interior Design; Surface Pattern Design; Design; Leather Tooling, Bookbinding, Metal Work; Lettering; Construction (such as toys, marionettes, etc.); Pencil Drawing; Ink Drawing; Crayon Drawing; Charcoal Drawing; Chalk or Pastel Drawing; Sculpture; and Ceramics.

A judge, from outside the State of North Carolina, is selected by the heads of the Art Departments. Many well-known art educators have served in this capacity. The list contains such names as Victor D'Amico, Director, Education Department of the Museum of Modern Art, New York City; Ray Faulkner, Head of the Department of Art, Teachers College, Columbia University; and Ralph Pearson, of the Pearson School of Design.

All work accepted for exhibition is retained by the Exhibition Committee for circulation as a travelling exhibit throughout the school year. Pupils and teachers are thus given an opportunity to see what is being done in other schools. The circulating exhibition acts as a stimulus to better art teaching and to improved art production. Women's clubs in the local communities help sponsor the exhibits.

In 1945 the exhibition was limited to the elementary schools. Since 1938 the North Carolina Federation of Women's Clubs has presented a certificate of award to all exhibitors whose work is selected for the exhibition. Each year the exhibition is shown in an increasing number of North Carolina cities and towns.

The Art Department also sponsors the circulation of many other exhibitions. In 1937 it acquired a collection of 70 enlargements of Miss Frances Benjamin Johnston's photographs of early North Carolina architecture, and a group of reproductions of famous paintings. These two collections were the nucleus of a number of circulating art exhibitions which have been loaned to schools and civic groups throughout the State.

The Art Department owns a collection consisting of many fine prints and reproductions which are loaned for a nominal rental fee. Many students and townspeople take advantage of this opportunity to have fine pictures in their homes and dormitory rooms.

During the last four years the Orange County Schools have used this rental service. A group of prints and reproductions are selected for the year to be loaned to the participating schools, on a monthly circuit schedule. At the beginning of the first month each school receives a picture, accompanied by mimeographed material about the artist and his subject. This material remains in the school a month and is used in each classroom for study and enjoyment. At the beginning of the next month a new print is received and the last one is sent to the next school as scheduled. In this way each class has experience with eight different prints during the school year.

The Parent-Teacher Associations have also used these prints for study while they were in the schools. Children and parents thus enjoy good art together.

Audio-Visual Education

While the "Magic Lantern" slide was still a mystery to many people, the Extension Division recognized it as a possible method of speeding up the learning process. Convinced that the eye makes possible detailed impressions upon the mind, enthusiasm for this method of instruction led to the establishment of the Bureau of Visual Instruction, in 1924.

Commercial companies had for many years marketed "stereoscopic views," and were rapidly turning their large collection of negatives into this new product, the lantern slide. Negatives which could justly be called educational, were limited to views of distant places and people and the resulting slides were related only to the teaching of history and geography. But such limitations in no way lessened enthusiasm. The Bureau acquired such slides as were available and began to circulate them not only to schools throughout the State, but to women's clubs, churches and other community organizations. Frequently mimeographed material accompanied a collection of slides, providing a lecture to be read while the slides were shown.

The possibilities of visual instruction were recognized by a rapid expansion of material covering many subjects. Science classes were soon able to see microscopic flower sections magnified to study proportions, and classes in rural economics had visualized for them the tragedies resulting from soil erosion.

The idea spread rapidly. Parent-Teacher Associations in many cases assumed the responsibility of financing the necessary projectors and equipment for such teaching. The demand for slides increased and the Bureau served as a depository for thousands of slides, thus making a large collection available to schools which would otherwise have access to only a limited number.

The motion picture film was the next step in progress. The history of the educational film runs parallel to that in the entertainment world. At first only the crude silent motion picture was available. Rapid improvements in production techniques quickly followed. Then the sound track was added and later color was made possible.

With each new development the Extension Division adjusted equipment, personnel and methods of distribution. Even the name was changed to include sound so now this material is handled by the Bureau of Audio-Visual Education.

The remarkable training records made by the Army and Navy have demonstrated the limitless possibilities of audio-visual aids. The idea of such instruction no longer has to be "sold" to the public. Several problems, however have to be met and continue to challenge those who desire to render a complete service to the schools and civic organizations of the State.

Distribution has from the beginning been a problem. Breakage, train and bus schedules and the irresponsibility of the human element has made schedules impossible many times thus discouraging would-be users. Distribution has also been curtailed by lack of equipment. Only schools with electricity, a projector and means of darkening the class room have been able to consider such teaching aids.

The rapidity with which schools are recognizing these items as standard teaching equipment is most encouraging. In many communities the equipment is purchased through co-operative means and is used by all civic groups. Circuits for distribution are proving highly satisfactory and as duplicate copies of titles are possible, schedules are more easily met.

Correct utilization is another matter to be understood before satisfactory teaching will be attained. Slides and films cannot be considered a short-cut to instruction. On the contrary, a teacher attempting to use educational films must develop a technique for handling such material and must be willing to devote hours to preparation previous to classroom showings. A definite effort to attain best results is being made. Films showing proper method of presentation have been made to aid the teacher in evaluating his own use of the material. Manuals for use accompany many films. Lectures and demonstrations are also held, upon request, for the training of teachers in this new teaching technique. Correct usage is one of the most important considerations in the development of an audio-visual aids program. The best film is of little value unless properly presented.

The third problem is the lack of an adequate supply of suitable films for teaching purposes. Having had their attention focused upon the possibilities of audio-visual aids during the war, many teachers are now seeking new materials. Regular users of films are finding some of the existing material faulty or inadequate. All known resources are now being utilized to meet this situation. The Head of the Bureau who has had experience in both the production and the use of teaching films, consults faculty members, school superintendents, and teachers, regarding their needs. He then contacts producers and distributors to procure the best available educational films. Teaching films produced by educational experts, to meet specific needs is the next step. The University plans to engage in the production of documentary and educational films in the near future.

The library of the Bureau of Audio-Visual Education now contains 2500 slides and approximately 1000 films. It also serves as a depository for films loaned by domestic and foreign organizations, thereby providing the people of the State authentic productions from many educational agencies at home and abroad.

Debating, Athletic, and Academic Contests

Each spring since 1913 the campus of the University of North Carolina has swarmed for three days with high school students who come from all parts of the State to participate in the annual debating contest. Clad in their new spring finery they present a gay and colorful cross-section of life in the State. Regardless of size, every accredited high school has an opportunity to compete for the Aycock Cup. Chapel Hill becomes debate conscious. The girls and their chaperones are entertained in the homes of the village while the boys share rooms with University men students in the dormitories and fraternity houses.

This assemblage marks the final episode in a statewide contest. Each local high school desiring to compete organizes a team for both the negative and affirmative side of the issue to be debated. All schools are then grouped in triangles, and the first elimination debates are held throughout the State. Each school whose negative and affirmative teams win in the triangular debating contests becomes eligible to enter the finals at Chapel Hill.

Upon arrival as guests at the University, further eliminations are held. On the last night, the best negative team meets the best affirmative team in the final debate which takes place before a large audience in Memorial Hall, the highly coveted Aycock Cup going to the school having the winning team.

This activity had its beginning in 1912 when the Dialectic and Philanthropic Literary Societies sponsored the organization of the North Carolina High School Debating Union. Their purpose was to awaken an interest in the discussion of important state, national, and international questions. Their funds proved insufficient to carry the project through so they appealed to the University for financial support. This was generously granted through the Bureau of Extension. The division of public discussion and debate assumed the responsibility of compiling a handbook to be used by the participants, and of making the preliminary arrangements. The first contest was held in 1913. Ninety schools debated the pros and cons of "Woman Suffrage." It is significant that the winning team came from Pleasant Garden, a farm-life school in Guilford County, which defeated the Durham High School in the final debate.

Each year, for many years, the number of schools participating increased. The cherished Aycock Cup has passed from Manteo to Murphy in its journey over the State, proving beyond question that a boy or girl from the village or rural district, if given an opportunity, can attain the same heights as one dwelling in an urban community.

The Head of the Bureau of High School Relations now handles all details connected with these annual debates. He compiles and publishes the Debate Handbook and serves as Executive Secretary of the High School Debating Union.

Shortly after the first statewide debate took place a request came for the same sort of organization in the field of high school athletics. A group of school superintendents and principals met with the University's head football coach. The foundation was laid for what later became the State High School Athletic Association, with the Head of the Bureau of High School Relations as its executive secretary. The purpose was to promote good sportsmanship through athletic competition in football, basketball, baseball, track, and other sports for the small village and consolidated school as well as for the large city school. All records and schedules were handled by the Extension office. State championship games were played on the University campus and attracted hundreds of supporters of the opposing teams.

Many changes have been made in the organization and in the regulations governing the contests. A member of the Extension

Division staff continues to serve as the executive secretary. The annual championship games are exciting events attended by thousands of people from all parts of the State. In recent years, due to wartime restrictions on travel, the championship games have been played away from Chapel Hill.

Academic contests for high school students were first held in 1925, in the subject of Latin. The following year saw the beginning of contests in French, Spanish, and Mathematics. In 1938 one was begun in Physics, and still later a contest in History was added. Each contest is organized with the cooperation of the University academic department concerned. All of these contests are held in the spring of the year.

The Extension Division publishes a bulletin early in the school year announcing the academic contests. As the date for each contest arrives, sealed envelopes containing the examinations are sent to all participating schools. At the appointed hour pupils all over the state are administered the same examination by the principal or teacher in charge. The papers are graded by the local teacher, who sends the three best to the University. Here they are graded by a faculty member representing the cooperating department. Public announcements are made of the schools whose students wins first, second or third places.

Drama

Perhaps no other Extension activity has touched closely so many people as that of the work of the Bureau of Community Drama. It has been the means of getting people to work creatively together, to play together, and to appreciate the work of others. Reaching into the most remote communities of the State it has found there the talent and material for the creation of lasting bits of drama which will help preserve for the State its rich folklore.

The history of the development of this work under the inspired leadership of "Proff" Koch is ably told in *Pioneering a People's Theatre*,* by Kai Heiberg-Jurgensen, under the title "Drama in Extension." Therefore this article will review only briefly the work as carried on at the present time.

The staff consists of the Head of the Department of Dramatic Art, who serves as Head of the Bureau, a secretary, and clerical assistants who fluctuate in number as the busy or slack seasons come and go. The Secretary of the Bureau also serves as Business Manager of the Carolina Playmakers.

At times the office runs with a degree of routine that belies the many-sided program being followed. But at other periods the rush and bustle bespeak the parade of events.

The purpose of the Bureau is "to promote and encourage dramatic art in the schools, colleges, and communities of North Carolina; to meet the need for a genuinely constructive recreation; to cooperate in the production of plays, pageants, and festivals of real worth, and to stimulate interest in the writing of native drama."

The machinery for attaining these aims includes advice in the selection of plays, consultant service in playwriting, play production, and technical problems involved, the writing of communal plays and pageants and the direction of their production, a package library service, a lecture service, extension courses for credit in play production, and the administration of the Carolina Dramatic Association.

The first of these activities runs on a fairly even keel through the year. The daily mail brings varied requests from all types of groups. Small schools needing help in the selection of the senior class play get the same personal consideration as the highly organized play production groups wanting aid in technical

---

* A Sesquicentennial publication, pp. 54-62

problems. Reference material for historical background or on all subjects relating to stagecraft and problems of production are sent in package libraries upon request. The Bureau Secretary serves as a booking agent and fills requests for lectures by scheduling staff members from the Dramatic Art Department. Requests for further training in the field of dramatic art are met by the organization of extension classes in play production. In cooperation with the Dramatic Art Department instructors are sent into the State and local leaders are given the opportunity to improve their talents while still "on the job." So successfully have these activities encouraged dramatic art in the schools, colleges, and communities of North Carolina that the work of the Carolina Dramatic Association involves a year-round program culminating in the Annual Dramatic Festival.

The cooperation of the Extension Division with this state organization is a fine example of the way the Univeristy serves the people throughout the State. When, in 1923, the school and community drama groups felt the need of an organization to foster their aims, they looked to the University for leadership, and the Carolina Dramatic Association was formed. Leadership was provided through the appointment of the Bureau Secretary as the Executive Secretary of the Association. The University assumed responsibility for salary, office space, and clerical help, thus giving financial assistance as well as professional guidance. Each year the Association sponsors contests in playwriting, play production, costume design, makeup, and originality of set design. Little theater groups and school units all over the State participate. Hundreds of plays are produced before local audiences, totaling thousands each year. Local groups hold playwriting contests and submit the best to the Bureau for selection and production in the State Drama Tournament.

As the time approaches for the Annual Dramatic Festival, which includes the final productions in the State Tournament, the office of the Secretary becomes a clearing house for details, and all available personnel is pressed into service. Each day telegrams arrive requiring changes in the program. Hourly the number of participants change, and rooms are either engaged or cancelled. Requests for certain types of stage equipment keep the stage manager busy lining up something new, in order that he may be ready when the players arrive. Each person has his responsibility, but the atmosphere of a "first night" covers all routine jobs with glamor and excitement. After judges have been secured, stage requirements met, rooming accommodations arranged, original plays selected for production, the programs printed, tickets placed on sale—the festival opens.

Each year they come in ever increasing numbers, bringing their best productions for presentation on the stage of The Playmakers Theatre. The enthusiast can satisfy his cravings. For three days the plays go on—comedy, tragedy, fantasy, folk plays, and sophisticated drama, plays written by professionals and by youthful amateurs. Each has its place in the parade of creative art and each is awarded a place according to its merit. The areas around the Theatre swarm with contestants in their costumes and make-up, giving the very campus an air of make-believe.

While the visiting groups are here, the Directors meet together for a "Directors Conference" to plan for future cooperation and expansion of the program.

Interest reaches its peak, when, on the last night of the Festival, the announcement of awards is made. It is a surprising and heart-warming experience to remember a play that has stirred you deeply with its understanding of human relationships, and then see the author, a young and wholesome youth, go forward to receive his award. Creative talent is being discovered and nurtured by the Carolina Dramatic Association. The Extension Division, through the Bureau of Community Drama, is proud of its part in this cultural activity.

When the Extension Division established its radio studio another opportunity for the extension of dramatic art was provided. Through the cooperation of the two departments, "The Carolina Playmakers of the Air" became regular broadcasters. Programs thus provided were carried over a national network.

These activities carried on by the Extension Division do not give a complete picture of all that is done by way of extending Dramatic Art beyond the confines of the University. No true picture could be obtained without mentioning what is done by the Dramatic Art Department itself. Chief among such activities is the annual Playmakers Tour. For many years the Carolina Playmakers have taken their productions over the State, showing what they are accomplishing in writing and production. These demonstrations help many local groups see the practical solution of technical problems. On several occasions these tours have covered a much wider territory. The Playmakers have appeared in cities and towns along the Atlantic seaboard and as far west as Texas. The most extensive tour was made in 1941 when "The House of Connolly" was presented on a Redpath circuit.

English

The Extension Division in cooperation with the University Department of English has developed a unique service for the English teachers of the State. With a faculty member of the English Department serving as Head of the Bureau, much help is given English teachers, both individually and as a group, throughout the year.

Working with the Department of English Teachers of the North Carolina Education Association, the Bureau Head has done much to bring about a renaissance among the English teachers of the State. Serving as the Executive Secretary of their Central Committee, his office has become the clearing house of source material and the fountainhead of inspiration as well as the workshop for planning, organizing and supervising committee work carried on by its members. The group has adopted the shorter title of "North Carolina English Teachers," and with much professional pride they are working on pertinent problems.

The work of the organization is carried on by the following committees: Committee on Professional Standards, with its sub-committees on Pre-Service Training and In-Service Training; Curriculum Committee; Committee on Teaching Load; Committee on Textbooks and Materials; and Committee on Research. The work of all committees is coordinated by an executive board called the Central Committee. It is through the Executive Secretary of this last Committee that the Extension Division provides its services.

A need was felt for a publication which would serve as a regular medium of communication among teachers of English. Such a publication appeared in April, 1943. It is a small leaflet, now published quarterly, which carries news of the work being done by various committees, specimens units of work, suggested book lists, questions for help, and general information about the organization and its members. At present the publication is sent to about 1200 teachers of English. Editorial work and details of printing are handled by the office of the Bureau of English Extension.

Another means of attacking their problems has been through the "High School English Institute." This institute, which is held for a three or four-week period, makes it possible for those in attendance to earn a maximum of 4½ semester hours of University credit. Under the leadership of the Head of the Bureau of English Extension, a program of study is prepared and executed which provides an opportunity to experience improved teaching techniques, evaluate materials and procedures, and receive help on specific individual problems. These institutes have attracted members from all sections of North Carolina and from eight other states.

The North Carolina English Teachers are also justly proud of their contribution to the *Language Arts Bulletin*, published by the State Department of Public Instruction. Stimulated by the results of the English Institute in 1943, they collected material suitable for curriculum improvement in grades nine through twelve. Units of study submitted by individual teachers were compiled for publication by the editorial committee. Interest shown in this activity was highly satisfactory. Many excellent units were received which lack of space prohibited using. In 1945 this new bulletin was published, but was in no way considered final.

The Curriculum Committee will discuss and revise units already included in the *Bulletin* with the view to improvement. Such revision, to be carried on by the Curriculum Committee, will be issued by the State Department in mimeographed form, thus providing continuous clarification and new ideas. In this way the teachers of English take the leadership in curriculum development based upon the needs of the time.

The Executive Secretary has aided in reviving district meetings and in the reorganization of local groups. A course in "The Teaching of High School English" is offered by correspondence so that in-service training may be continued.

Such cooperation between the English Teachers and the Extension Division is typical of the way in which the University supplies professional leadership to raise standards in the public schools.

LECTURES AND LECTURE COURSES

From Battle's *History of the University* we learn that as early as 1880 the President and many faculty members made educational addresses throughout the State. Ever since that time, schools and community organizations have looked to the University for speakers on a wide variety of subjects.

In 1913-1914, the newly created Bureau of Extension increased this service to the State by organizing a lecture division. Each year a bulletin was published giving the names of available speakers and their topics. Many of these were travel talks illustrated by the use of stereoptican slides. Some years as many as 150 subjects were listed. Members of the faculty were most generous in giving lectures in all parts of the State. No fee was paid the lecturer but his expenses were met by the group issuing the invitation. During this time alumni of the University were particularly active in organizing lectures and lecture series, thus bringing to their communities men who had inspired them during their college days.

In 1921 the Bureau of Extension became a Division and the Lecture Division became the Bureau of Lectures and Short Courses. The change in name did not change its purpose, and we find the following announcement in Vol. I, No. 1 of *The University of North Carolina Extension Bulletin*: "Lectures: Popular or technical lectures, individual or in series for clubs and community organizations. Addresses for commencement or other special occasions. Write for lecture bulletin." More and more schools and colleges used this lecture service for securing commencement speakers. It is a tribute to the value of the service when in the spring of the year schools start closing, all available speakers are engaged.

Some faculty members have created a demand for their services as lecturers to such an extent that it is necessary to charge a nominal fee. Others still give generously of their

SCHOOL AND COMMUNITY ACTIVITIES 75

time carrying the spirit of the University to the people of the State. Booking arrangements are made through the Extension Division, and while complete records are not available it may be conservatively estimated that the average yearly attendance at these lectures is from twenty to thirty thousand.

Music

The Bureau of Community Music, organized in 1921 was an outgrowth of numerous requests for help that came from all parts of the State. Originally the requests were almost entirely for aid in the holding of "community sings." Filling these requests started a chain of events that has carried music to many local communities and has brought people from the communities to the campus for special assistance and training.

Instructors going into a town to help with the "sing" charged no fee for their services, but the expenses incurred were borne by the group making the request. Impetus thus gained was usually carried over into the formation of a community chorus under the guidance of University leadership. Interest in music spread, and all types of civic groups made use of the lecture and demonstration service offered through the Bureau.

Public schools were urged by community leaders to offer music courses. Few teachers were prepared to handle the subject. A cooperative arrangement was worked out with the Music Department and the Department of Education whereby a full-time instructor was employed and sent into the field by the Extension Division. She organized and taught classes in public school music throughout the State. Teachers were allowed credit for the courses and many communities were helped in meeting their needs for this type of instruction.

Closely following this activity came a statewide interest in high school orchestras and bands. Again the University through the Extension Division was able to help. Since 1935 boys and girls of high school age have been coming to the campus for a six-weeks course in music each summer. Regular classes are held in music theory, appreciation, and chamber music. The Band and Orchestra rehearse daily, and sectional rehearsals are held in woodwind, brass, and string ensembles. Each student receives one private lesson weekly. By special arrangement with the State Department of Public Instruction, one unit of music credit is granted for the successful completion of the course and this is recognized by all high schools in the State.

The Bureau has maintained an advisory service. Members of the faculty of the Music Department give freely of their time to the consideration of the music needs of local communities. They are consulted regarding the planning of programs, the purchase of instruments, the employment of teachers, and many other problems arising in the field of music.

A number of piano, violin, voice and organ recitals have been arranged upon request. University responsibilities and travel limitations have, however, greatly limited the area which may be served in this way. With the coming of radio, the remotest corner of the State can now enjoy such concerts. Through regularly scheduled broadcasts the Music Department now offers planned programs whereby interested listeners may enjoy the equivalent of a music course. Instructions to listeners are provided through mimeographed material sent out in advance. The success of one such series has created a demand for other programs.

The Music Department cooperates closely with all other departments in the use of radio and plays an important part in providing continuity for many broadcasts.

The University Glee Clubs make annual trips into the State and thus extend the work of the Department. The large audiences that attend these concerts are indicative of an increasing interest in good music in North Carolina.

Public Forums

Public discussion has been a major concern of University Extension since its beginning in 1912. Believing that the people of the State should discuss public affairs intelligently, every effort has been made to stimulate interest in current topics and to supply material for discussion groups. The University Library has cooperated most generously in the preparation of bibliographies and in mailing package libraries. Adult groups have maintained a steady interest. In 1940 public discussion in North Carolina received great impetus through assistance given by the United States Office of Education.

To help people help themselves in understanding rapidly changing world events, the United States Office of Education established a program of Public Forums. The University was selected as the North Carolina institution to carry out this program and the Extension Division became the administrative agency. The purpose was, "to stimulate study and discussion of public affairs as a means of extending civic knowledge and of strengthening democracy."

The Division received financial aid from the U. S. Office of Education and the close cooperation of the State Department of Public Instruction. The office of the Associate Director became the State Forum Office and he became the Director of Forums. He travelled extensively throughout the State to stimulate interest in adult civic education and to organize forum activities in the communities.

The results were satisfactory, both in the extent and in the spirit of the forums. One hundred and forty-three public forums were held with an attendance of 26,442, as follows: 84 community civic forums, 22 demonstration forums, and 37 radio forums. In addition to the forums as such, 42 meetings of civic clubs, parent-teacher associations, local, district, and state education associations heard addresses on the forum and adult civic education by the State Forum Director. Approximately 90 local conferences were held between the Director and community committees and councils.

Radio forums were carried regularly as a part of the University's radio service over the facilities of six stations.

The Director of Forums compiled a Forum Directory listing the names of 98 leaders and 336 separate topics covering a wide range of public affairs. The directory was constantly extended by the addition of both names and subjects for discussion.

All of this work was made more effective by the Information Center established in the University Library. Here, all the latest publications on current topics were made available. Forum leaders throughout the State soon learned to depend upon this Center for up-to-the-minute material on all subjects.

The program was temporarily interrupted by the loss of personnel when many of the local leaders joined the armed forces. Problems of reconversion and world peace now make the need for free discussion a necessity to the maintenance of our democracy.

PUBLICATIONS

From the time the Bureau of Extension was first created, and committed to the ideal of sharing the information accumulated at the University, with the people of the State, the distribution of printed material has been a factor of prime importance. Through the years the form and emphasis of such printed material have changed to meet the needs of the times.

Only one publication has retained its original purpose and format. *The News Letter* is today the same five column clipsheet it started out to be in 1914. Under the leadership of Professor E. C. Branson, head of the Department of Rural Economics and Sociology, the country life studies of North Carolina were begun. These studies accumulated quantities of data applicable to the problems of North Carolinians throughout the State. In order to make these facts available to all the people, the material was carefully digested and published in *The News Letter*. Starting November 17, 1914 with a mailing list of 3,500 its circulation has reached as high as 20,000 copies per issue. Professor S. H. Hobbs has carried on the late Professor Branson's editorship. He continues to pack *The News Letter* with social and economic facts relative to life in the State. Respect for this publication is reflected in the fact that editorial comment is frequently based on the information it contains, so that the results of research are given state-wide publicity.

As work of the Bureau of Extension progressed, new channels were needed to inform the people of the State concerning available services and to distribute requested information. The avenue for such publication was already open in *The University of North Carolina Record*. The Record was published by the University eight times a year. The Bureau of Extension was permitted to use issues of this publication for its own purpose. Beginning in 1913, the Bureau started the *Extension Series*, which ran for eight years as publications of *The Record*. Forty-one bulletins were published in this manner. A short listing of selected titles will indicate the variety of groups served:

"A Library for Teachers"
"Correspondence Instruction"
"Collective Bargaining"—Debate Handbook
"The North Carolina Club Yearbook"
"The Good Roads Institute."

In 1920 when the Bureau of Extension was reorganized to become the University Extension Division, many other changes occurred, among which was the merging of *The Extension Series* with *The Extension Leaflets* into a new publication which is now known as *The University of North Carolina Extension Bulletin*.

The *Bulletin* carries the imprint of the University of North Carolina Press and is entered as second-class matter. The first seven volumes of the *Bulletin* contained fourteen issues, but this has gradually been reduced to six. Until 1934, six issues were annually assigned to the Extension Library to be used for the publication of outlines for individual and group study. This series is now published by the Library Extension Department of the University Library under the name *The University of North Carolina Library Extension Publication*.

The purpose of the *Bulletin* has always been the same. It is the media by which the Division keeps the public informed of available services and is also the means of publishing requested material. In recent years, the following titles have appeared:

"University Lectures" (Announcement of Lecture Bureau Services)
"The Rural Playground," by H. D. Meyer
"Relativity—A Romance of Sciences," by Archibald Henderson
"Children of Old Carolina," An Historical Pageant, by Ethel T. Rockwell
"A Handbook for N. C. Parent-Teacher Associations"
"Debate Handbook"

A pattern of publication has gradually been developed. Each year an issue is devoted to debating, science, drama, economic and social studies, and announcements. As emergencies have arisen and public interests varied, the pattern has changed; but its purpose, service to the people, has remained constant.

The Extension Leaflet came into being in 1915-1916 along with a small publication known as *Extension Bureau Circulars*. The *Leaflet* was small, as its name would indicate, and served to announce courses as the first three titles show:

"Courses with University Credit"
"Courses for Teachers"
"Courses for Workers"

The following year brought World War I and the *Leaflet* assumed a new role. It became the media for circulating war information and facts concerning national problems. The 1918-1919 titles are startlingly similar to those appearing during World War II:

"Why Are We at War With Germany?"
"What to Read Concerning the Great War"
"Will You Keep the Freedom Our Soldiers Win?"
"America and Her Allies"

The *Leaflet* served well through the war years and the readjustment period, but by 1921 it had fulfilled its purpose and was wisely merged with the *Record*.

The *Extension Bureau Circulars* which came into being the same year as the *Leaflet* are still in existence, although they too have undergone many changes. The first series has such titles as: "Our Country Church Problems," "Our Carolina Highlanders," and "Wealth, Welfare, and Willingness in North Carolina," which would indicate they were first issued to discuss community problems of our rural districts. In 1921 the word Bureau was dropped, and the name became *Extension Circular*. It was then used to announce activities of the Division such as athletic contests and coaching schools. In 1926 the name was changed again. This time it was called *The University of North Carolina Extension News* but has been most frequently referred to as simply *Extension News*. It is a six page folder announcing services of the Division. In this respect it differs from the bulletin announcements in that it is more specific, giving details of service to a limited group in a special field. The following titles illustrate this point:

"Training for Parenthood"
"Economical Plans for College and Adult Education"
    (of special interest to high school graduates)
"The 15th Annual Coaching School"
"Outlines of Study and Directed Reading" (Women's Clubs)

"Statewide Program of Adult Education"
"Summer School Institutes"

During the period between December 1923 and June 1926, the School of Commerce, through the Bureau of Commercial and Industrial Relations, sponsored a publication known as *North Carolina Commerce and Industry*. Each issue carried statistical studies with comparisons and interpretations concerning the commercial progress of the State.

A small leaflet called *The English Teacher* is published quarterly. It first appeared in April 1943 and serves as a medium of communication among teachers of English.

In like manner, *The Bulletin of the North Carolina Council for the Social Studies* is published by the Division in cooperation with the social science teachers of the State.

New trends in educational thinking lead to new activities in extension, and they in turn create a need for new publications. The Division will continue, through its publications, in so far as its resources will permit, to make available the results of research, study, and laboratory experiments to all the people of the State.

Radio

Long before the University established its own radio studio, regular programs were broadcast through the courtesy of radio stations in Durham and Raleigh. Through the cooperation of these stations two plans for broadcasting were made possible, depending upon the type of program to be presented. Lecturers, round table speakers, and small entertainment groups went to the studio which was to broadcast the program. Concerts, or public lectures given by nationally known speakers, on the campus were picked up by a direct line from the hall in which they were given and broadcast by the cooperating station.

These two plans were appreciated for they enabled the University to share its resources with the people of the State. The Music Department presented a series of Sunday afternoon concerts. The Department of Dramatic Art broadcast one act plays, and several lecture courses were given in the fields of history, commerce, and political science. Courses were given in French and Spanish. Such arrangements also made possible the broadcasting of special events such as The Orange County Music Festival, and the Town Hall of the Air.

Problems of rehearsals, transportation and administration were numerous. The next step was to acquire a studio which would permit small groups to have their programs carried by direct wire as concerts and public gatherings are carried. The studio would also permit training in many technical problems and provide suitable rehearsal space.

The University's first adventure in radio broadcasting from its own studio took place in 1940. In May of that year, under the direction of the Associate Director of the Extension Division, the Radio Studio in Caldwell Hall was officially dedicated. It was doomed to a short existence. By 1942, due to lack of space, the equipment had been put into packing boxes for "the duration." However, in that short period Radio had become an important factor in extending the resources of the University to the people of the State.

In his report, the Head of the Radio Department made this statement: "The primary aim of all University radio programs is to render educational service to the people of the State; a secondary objective is to provide practical training in radio for faculty members and students. An indirect outcome, not set up as an objective at all, is a more intimate relationship between the University and the people of North Carolina. The radio literally makes the boundaries of the University campus coterminus with the boundaries of the State."

The official staff of the Radio Department, which developed gradually during the first year of broadcasting, reached the total of 42 persons serving variously as directors of programs, announcers, technicians, writers, secretaries, and production assistants. A few of these people were part-time employes, but most of them were faculty members and students whose services were voluntary. More than 300 faculty members and students of the University participated in the radio broadcasts.

Programs were produced by representatives of several university departments and students organizations. Programs of the following types were broadcast: glee club, band and symphony orchestra concerts; music recitals and ensembles; programs depicting the work of various University departments and organizations; plays; lessons in North Carolina History; Carolina Political Union forums; special events at the University, such as commencement and student-faculty day; book reviews; science talks; philosophy round tables; weekly news summaries; "Our American Neighbors," programs to describe life in the other American nations; journalistic interviews; lectures and addresses on a variety of subjects.

The estimated weekly listening audience for the University radio programs was a minimum of half a million people. The reaching of so large a number of persons with the educational services of the University was a result of a unique plan of cooperation between the University and the commercial stations in the State, an arrangement described by the Chairman of the Federal Communications Commission as "ideal." The University had the cooperation of the following eleven stations: WDNC Durham; WPTF Raleigh; WRAL Raleigh; WBIG Greensboro; WGTM Wilson; WFTC Kinston; WSTP Salisbury; WSJS Winston-Salem; WAIR Winston-Salem; WSOC Charlotte; the affiliated Mutual station at Greenville, South Carolina.

Under the direction of Mr. Earl Wynn, the Playmakers of the Air broadcast a series of six original plays over the nation wide facilities of the Mutual Broadcasting System, reaching an audience of many millions each week.

New quarters have now been acquired and a modest beginning made for the re-establishment of radio at the University, with plans well underway for a Frequency Modulation educational station and other new developments of this media of communication.

RECREATION

Through the years the University Extension Division has recognized the place of recreation in community life and has made significant contributions to the promotion of recreation not only in North Carolina but throughout the South. The Bureau of Recreation, an integral part of the Extension Division, was established in 1923 and has been rendering service since that time. It was established in cooperation with the Sociology Department under the leadership of Professor Harold D. Meyer.

The services which this Bureau has rendered may be briefly described as follows:

Relation to Communities. Here the Bureau has functioned by direct services to communities in a consultative and advisory capacity. Meetings have been held with hundreds of community groups representing public officials, private agencies and commercial organizations. Recreation departments have been established, programs have been set up, areas and facilities designed and located, problems of leadership personnel worked out, and public relations promoted.

Bulletins and Other Publications. Through the years the Bureau has published many bulletins relating to recreation and has sent out literally thousands of leaflets, rental libraries and other information relating to recreation activities.

Extension Courses. Recognizing the need for trained recreation leadership, both on the professional and volunteer levels, extension courses in recreation have been established and taught in many communities throughout the State. Here have gathered together workers for refresher courses, in-service training, and general training in the field. This is one illustration of the University reaching out to the people in practical training opportunities.

Correspondence Instruction. As another aid in the training program, correspondence courses are available in the field of recreation and hundreds of leaders have taken the courses as an effective means to better leadership and a better understanding of recreational techniques. Hundreds of teachers have taken the courses enriching the recreational program of the schools.

Surveys and Studies. Many surveys and studies have been made of local communities, districts and counties. These surveys and studies have aided communities in understanding the recreational picture, planning for progressive growth, bringing about better coordination of existing services, and establishing a factual basis for future planning. Emphasis has been given to administration and organization, program building, areas and facilities, finances, and leadership.

Institutes, Conferences, and Workshops. In the span of years the Bureau has held hundreds of recreation institutes, conferences, and workshops on and off the campus. These meetings have been of all types—professional groups, volunteer workers, specific programs for industrial recreation leaders, recreation in rural areas, recreation for church workers, and the like.

Addresses. The Bureau has served many national, state, and local organizations in making talks to members. Parent-

Teacher Associations, units of the Federation of Women's Clubs, educational groups, home and farm demonstration meetings, civic groups of all types, fraternal orders and religious organizations are among some of the classifications served.

Youth Services. With a continuous interest in youth, the Bureau has worked very closely with numerous national, state, and local youth groups in furthering the work of these organizations. The Boy Scouts of America, Camp Fire Girls, Girl Scouts, Boys' Clubs of America, 4-H Clubs, young peoples' religious groups, student government organizations, YMCA, YWCA and many others have received assistance and service in many ways.

In addition to these services there has been constant contact with individuals and organizations through correspondence. Every effort is made within the limits of time and facilities to render effective service to the State and the South in the building of better recreational opportunities for the masses of the people.

Through the war period the Bureau acted as Coordinator for Recreation in the Office of Civilian Defense and served many military units located in the State.

The North Carolina Recreation Commission. The uses of, the benefits from, and the needs for recreation are constantly on the increase. Recognizing this fact, the leadership of the University Extension Division has taken an active part in the organization of the North Carolina Recreation Commission, which was established by the General Assembly of North Carolina in 1945, the first of its kind in the United States. The Chief of the Bureau is acting as Director of the Commission and the Director of the University Extension Division is serving as Chairman of the Commission's Advisory Committee.

V

COOPERATION WITH STATE, REGIONAL, AND NATIONAL ORGANIZATIONS

COOPERATION WITH STATE, REGIONAL AND NATIONAL ORGANIZATIONS

The Extension Division, with its broad interpretation of the term "Adult Education," logically represents the University in its off-campus contacts with individuals and organized groups or agencies. Wherever the need for educational services presents itself, an effect is made to render assistance.

Frequently the University, through the Extension Division, takes the initiative in offering services to organized groups. At other times an organization may approach the University seeking help with a definite problem, or, the University may solicit the cooperation of an organization in the development of a program.

The willingness to cooperate in the development of constructive programs and to help in carrying such programs to a successful conclusion has been of mutual benefit. The University has established its reputation for leadership and impartiality, denying to none the right to profit by the advantages it has to offer.

Taking its place as one of the leading universities of the nation, such working relationships are not limited to the State, but are extended to regional and national organizations.

Probably the simplest examples of such cooperation are found in the conferences at which the University serves only as the host institution. The University with its atmosphere of culture and the campus with its natural beauty make Chapel Hill a desirable meeting place for groups wishing to combine comfort, beauty and inspiration. As a result, the University is annually asked to be host to many organizations wishing to use the facilities of the University for their state, regional or national meetings. The Extension Division, acting as representative for the University, becomes responsible for all local details of housing, feeding and transportation. Interested departments are invited to participate, but assume little or no responsibility. Frequently the only connection with the University, other than the services rendered by the Extension Division, is the greeting of welcome extended by some member of the administration.

Such visitors vary from year to year. During the War it was necssary to limit the number in attendance. Housing difficulties now impose restrictions. In the past a single national society brought as many as 2800 guests. The Division looks forward to the time when such activities may be resumed without limitations.

The following list, which is by no means complete, serves to show the type of organizations served:

    Business and Professional Women's Club Institute
    Conference on Public Forums
    Convention of the American Chemical Society
    Junior Red Cross Workshop
    National Academy of Science
    North Carolina Photographers Association
    Post Office Clerks and Letter Carriers' Convention
    Southern Training Institute T.W.U.A.
    Summer Institute of the North Carolina Federation of Women's Clubs

In contrast to this type of co-operation, which is of short duration and involves little more than meeting physical needs, are the yearly working arrangements which exist between the University and many organized groups. In some instances such co-operation began as early as 1913 and has continued to the present time. Some have been interrupted by national emergencies. Others have only recently been established and are an outgrowth of new trends in extension service.

In explaining such relationships it is impractical to trace the working agreements which have developed in every case.

A few that have continued for many years have been selected as examples. Descriptions of several of these cooperative relationships have been given in Chapters II and IV.

State Organizations
North Carolina Congress of Parents and Teachers

The resolutions adopted by the 1946 annual convention of the North Carolina Congress of Parents and Teachers contained the following statement: "Be it resolved, that the North Carolina Congress of Parents and Teachers does extend greetings and felicitations to the University of North Carolina upon the occasion of the celebration of its one hundred and fiftieth anniversary.

"Cognizant of the great place that the University has had in the building of our State and of the tremendous service it has rendered to the culture of North Carolina, the Congress of Parents and Teachers would take this occasion to commend it particularly for the aid and encouragement it has given to the public schools through the education of young men and women as teachers and parents of our youth; through the loan of its faculty as speakers and advisers; through the extension of its material facilities for programs and meetings; and for the recognition and enthusiastic encouragement it has given to all organizations and movements for the education and the development of youth.

"For all this, the North Carolina Congress of Parents and Teachers is duly grateful, and it would pray for the University of North Carolina a continuing future of service and an ever affectionate place in the hearts of the people of the State."

Such a statement of affection and gratitude was not mere form, but was an outgrowth of sincere appreciation for leadership and cooperation which the Congress has continuously received from the University, through the Extension Division, for the past twenty-seven years.

Since its beginning in 1919, the Extension Division has been glad to encourage and promote the objectives of the organization. Realizing that the success of the State program depended upon community participation, one of the first contributions made by the Division was the publication "The Parent-Teacher Handbook." This contained step-by-step proceedures for the organization of a local organization of the North Carolina Congress of Parents and Teachers. It was most gratefully received by those who believed in the cause but who had had little or no experience in the PTA activities. It made possible the organization of hundreds of local associations and was a contributing factor to the successful beginnings of the state organization. The popularity of the Handbook continued for several years, necessitating four subsequent editions.

Faculty members became members of standing committees and helped formulate policies and programs. Since the beginning, such names as Graham, Teague, Phillips, Meyer, Groves and Grumman have run through their literature and Institute programs. The Library Extension Service established a special collection of books pertinent to Parent-Teacher work. These are loaned to local associations for their study groups and guidance programs.

One of the first state-wide efforts to foster art in the public schools was sponsored by the Congress of Parents and Teachers. Through local associations children were encouraged to enter a Poster Contest. The Extension Division cooperated by attending to all the details of conducting the contest, furnishing the judges and handling all correspondence.

The growth of the Congress was rapid and by 1928 the need for trained leadership led to the establishment of the annual Parent-Teacher Institute, at Chapel Hill. The Institute is primarily for in-coming officers and the program is so arranged as to provide instruction in the general program of Parent-Teacher cooperation, the objectives of the organization, and the individual responsibility of each officer. The Director of Extension was made the director of the first Institute and continued to carry that responsibility until 1942 when crowded conditions on the campus made it necessary to move the Institute to the Woman's College at Greensboro. The University, through its Director of Extension at that institution, continues to provide the same leadership.

In 1934 the Congress decided that the needs of local associations could best be met by means of a Field Representative, who would travel over the State giving personalized consideration to local problems. The Director of Extension was appointed chairman of a committee to work out the details of such a plan. A woman who had had many years of Parent-Teacher experience was employed for the position. The Extension office circularized the fact that her services were available and received requests. It made out her schedule and arranged her transportation. The work of the Field Representative changed as associations matured. At present one feature which is indicative of the prestige being gained by the organization is the cooperation with the colleges. This includes visitation work at the summer schools and at classes in education at teacher-training institutions. Prospective teachers are thus introduced to Parent-Teacher Association principles and objectives.

The work of the Field Representative is now handled in the office of an Executive Secretary, which is further indication of the growth of the organization.

A History of the North Carolina Congress of Parents and Teachers, Volume I, covering the period 1919-1944, gives a comprehensive review of the activities of the organization, and traces the contributions made to it by the Extension Division.

NORTH CAROLINA STATE BOARD OF HEALTH

Cooperative relationships between the State Board of Health and the Extension Division were established as early as 1916. In that year the first post-graduate medical course was organized.* Since that time the Extension Division has continuously offered its services for the promotion of public health in the State.

Annual summer school courses have been provided for dentists engaged in public health service to broaden their understanding of child psychology and school problems. The Bureau of Community Drama has cooperated with the Division of Oral Hygiene in sponsoring puppet shows for the teaching of the proper care of the teeth. An automobile equipped with the necessary stage equipment has toured the State with this "visual aid" to health education.

For several summers, the School-Health Coordinating Service, which represents both the State Board of Health and the State Department of Public Instruction has conducted a Child Health Conference for teachers at Chapel Hill. The Extension Division has given assistance to this program, particularly in the field of Special Education, *i.e.*, the teaching of the hard-of-hearing and the physically handicapped groups. A laboratory school is operated as part of the six weeks conference.

At the request of the Coordinating Service, the Extension Division has offered credit courses on "The Problems of the Mal-adjusted Child" at many centers throughout the State.

As the campaign for public health becomes recognized as everyman's problem, the opportunities to serve are expanded. Plans for further classes and public instruction in the conservation of health are now being formulated. The Extension Division solicits the cooperation of all University departments

---

* See Post-Graduate Medical and Dental Courses.

NORTH CAROLINA STATE DEPARTMENT OF PUBLIC INSTRUCTION

which can assist in this work and offers this service to the State Board of Health.

The first extension activity, recorded as such, was developed in cooperation with the State Department of Public Instruction. In 1913 Dr. Louis R. Wilson offered the resources of the University library to the people of the State. Professor Nathan W. Walker, who, at that time, was State Inspector of High Schools, took advantage of this offer to supplement the reading of high school pupils. Since that time extension service has been adjusted and expanded to meet the changing needs of the public schools as interpreted by the State Department of Public Instruction.

The work carried on may be classified in three distinct types: courses given for credit to meet the requirements of the state program of teacher certification; institutes, conferences and workshops held for professional study and improvement; and programs conducted for school pupils to supplement opportunities offered by the local schools.

The Division of Certification establishes specific requirements which all teachers must meet before employment or advancement is secured. The correspondence courses and extension class instruction offered by the Extension Division in cooperation with the Education Department, make it possible for teachers to continue their professional growth while in service. Courses carrying University credit, with certain restrictions, are accepted by the State Department and may be applied toward raising or renewing teachers' certificates. The Extension Division maintains a counseling service for teachers who desire help in the selection of courses. The head of the Division of Certification and the Director of the Extension Division work closely together in order that the needs of teachers may be met. These courses offered through Extension at times and places, where most needed, have contributed greatly to the high teacher-training index prevailing in the State today. As standards have been raised, extension teaching service has shifted its emphasis from the undergraduate to the graduate level of instruction.

Institutes, conferences and workshops for teachers and school officials have long been utilized as techniques for improving the quality of teaching and school administration. To describe all of these cooperative adventures would be repetitions but the following will serve to illustrate the type of training offered:

The Division of Instructional Service of the State Department of Public Instruction organized a short summer course to stimulate interest and to promote active participation in art in the public schools. The Extension Division worked with the State Department in obtaining suitable lecturers and teachers. The course was given at Blue Ridge, N. C., and a representative of the Extension Division served as coordinator, making schedules and attending to administrative details.

The State Supervisor of School Libraries held a conference for school librarians at Chapel Hill. The Extension Division handled the necessary local arrangements for accommodating such a visiting group.

In the depression years when the Federal Emergency Relief Administration was organized, all state departments of education were asked to hold training courses for leaders and teachers in various fields of adult education. The Extension Division held several of these courses, including: the training course for State Supervisors of Adult Elementary Education, the training course for Supervisors of Worker's Education, and the training course for Recreation Workers. These were followed by conferences and institutes, held throughout the State under the direction of the Division in cooperation with the F.E.R.A. and the State Department.

University Extension programs conducted for school pupils, and designed to supplement opportunities offered by local schools, have steadily increased in range of interest and participation. Recognizing the fact that limited enrollment and financial support curtail many desirable educational experiences, the State Department of Public Instruction has cooperated with University departments and the Extension Division in making a few such opportunities available to the public school students of the State.

The Art Department working with these other agencies has for several years sponsored art contests and art exhibits for both elementary and high school boys and girls. Through this means art instruction has been vitalized in many schools.

At the request of the State Superintendent of Public Instruction the Journalism Department cooperates in sponsoring the North Carolina Scholastic Press Institute. This is an annual event for high schools having their own school papers. It is an effort to evaluate and raise the standards of such publications. Contests in format, editorials, and general content do much to supplement a school's program in English, citizenship, and art, as well as in journalism.

In 1935 the Music Department, in cooperation with the Extension Division, offered the first All State High School Music Course. Boys and girls from all over the State gathered on the University campus for six weeks to study Music Theory, Appreciation and for practice in Band and Orchestra. The State Department cooperated with this venture and approved the course for high school credit.

During the ten-year period this course has been offered, registrations have more than doubled. The stimulus thus given to hundreds of promising young musicians, and to music appreciation throughout the State can not be over emphasized.

The success of the music course paved the way for the development of a similar course in Dramatic Art. This course also carries high school credit. Dr. J. Henry Highsmith, Head of the Division of Instructional Service of the State Department, serves as consultant.

REGIONAL ORGANIZATIONS

As a result of the reputation which the University of North Carolina has established, requests are frequently received to aid in the promotion of educational projects fostered by regional agencies. The Extension Division is frequently called upon to represent the University in such matters of cooperation.

The Southern Council on International Relations is perhaps the most representative of these regional services and will therefore be described fully. Several others, however, deserve to be mentioned with a notation regarding the type of cooperation given.

Southeastern Association for Adult Education: The Director of the Extension Division was asked by the American Association for Adult Education to assume the leadership in founding the Southeastern Association. He has served as its President and is at present Secretary-Treasurer of the organization. He served as program chairman at its last annual meeting and is a member of the Executive Committee.

Southeastern Folklore Society: The Director of Extension has represented the University on the Executive Board of the Society and has served as its Secretary-Treasurer.

Southeastern Area American Red Cross: The Extension Division has served as Coordinator for the Regional Work Shop for Junior Red Cross Chairmen. It has sponsored two "Training Courses for Teachers of Home Nursing" and several "Training Courses for Swimming Instructors."

THE SOUTHERN COUNCIL ON INTERNATIONAL RELATIONS

The Southern Council on International Relations is a regional agency of the Carnegie Endowment for International Peace and is financed chiefly by means of an annual grant from that organization. The Office of the Coordinator of Inter-American Affairs, and the University of North Carolina have, in recent years, cooperated financially and otherwise with the Council. It is an organization of members from ten southern states established as a coordinating agency to promote adult education and action in international relations.

To carry out these aims, the Council maintains an office which serves as a source of information and help to all local communities interested in a better understanding of world problems. This office receives quantities of literature published by national and international agencies. These materials are mailed to study groups in the ten participating states. The Council, through its director, aids in the organization of local councils, and maintains a guidance service in the planning of programs and community projects. Art exhibitions, open forums, lectures, motion picture showings, and press releases are some of the techniques used to stimulate interest in and to clarify international issues. Whenever there is a sufficient demand for more formalized instruction, extension classes and correspondence courses are provided.

The Council directed the North Carolina Lecture-Institute Program for the Office of the Coordinator of Inter-American Affairs. This program served hundreds of schools, colleges, and communities and brought into the State as speakers such well known authorities on Latin America as Guy B. Inman, Hubert Herring, and John Harvey Furbay.

The magazine, *The South and World Affairs*, is published monthly by the Southern Council. This publication, devoted to "the South's place in the World," carries articles of current interest written by authorities. The effect of international policies upon the people of this region are frankly discussed. Reading lists which cover both sides of debatable questions are included.

President Graham served as Chairman of the Southern Council on International Relations for several years. Professor Keener C. Frazer, a member of the staff of the Department of Political Science, serves as Secretary and Director. During 1944-1945, the salary of a full-time director was paid jointly by The Carnegie Endowment for International Peace and the Extension Division. Office space and secretarial assistance were also provided by the Division. The Division cooperates with the Council in the distribution of motion picture films, lantern slides, and exhibits. Extension Library Service is made available to individuals and to local council groups.

NATIONAL ORGANIZATIONS

Most national organizations are dependent upon the cooperation of state and local agencies to carry out their aims, purposes, and programs. Without understanding and participation on the community level, little is accomplished on the national level. In like manner, much is gained by the local agency when its efforts are coordinated with nationwide activities. Through the Extension Division the University is able to participate in the planning of many nationwide movements and have a part in building programs of national importance.

The many groups with which the Extension Division works fall into three classes: first, national organizations and societies; second, federal agencies; and third, endowments and foundations established for research and educational development.

In the first group are such organizations as the National Education Association, the National University Extension Association, the American Association for Adult Education and many others. By representation on executive boards and planning committees the University contributes to the policy making of each organization and at the same time has the advantage of exchange of thought with the leaders in a given field throughout the nation.

Cooperation with federal agencies provides one of the greatest opportunities the University has to implement the programs of national scope. The United States Office of Education has turned repeatedly to the University for local interpretation and practice of its programs. Public forums sponsored by the Office offer an excellent example of how the University through the Extension Division makes possible the success of such a program.* On the other hand, the assistance given the Inter-American Institute is an illustration of how the United States Office of Education cooperates with a University program. The film service of the U. S. Department of Agriculture and other federal agencies is being channelled in North Carolina through the University's Bureau of Visual Education. The opportunities for mutual benefit coming from such cooperation are many.

The United States Employment Service turned to the University for aid in conducting its system of Merit Examinations. Through the Extension Division the University provided administrative direction, office space and clerical help for this national program which had to be carried out on the state level. Qualifications for employment were determined on three points, application, examination, and personal interview. The Extension Division staff under the supervision of a national representative scored the applications and corrected the examinations. The examining boards which toured the State conduct-

---

* See Public Forums.

ing personal interviews were composed of one representative from the national office, one representative from a neutral state and one faculty member from the University. In this case the University was able to contribute materially to the development of a national program of great service to the citizens of the State.

During the depression many national emergency programs came into being. Their efficiency was entirely dependent upon local execution. Many of these programs were of short duration but while they were in action the Extension Division did much to interpret their aims, train their leaders and house their oficials.

The State Educational Director of the CCC program was given office space by the Extension Division and for over a year conducted all the educational activities of that organization from the campus. He freely used staff and faculty members for the promotion of the national ideal set up by this agency.

Conferences, short courses, and training programs were provided for the leaders of FERA, WPA, PWA, CCC and FHA. All of these national programs became more effective in the State because of the leadership provided by the University.

National agencies which came into being during the second World War received similar cooperation. These have been discussed in detail in the chapter on University Extension in Wartime.

Many national foundations which are established for the furthering of research, educational opportunities, and international understanding, are also dependent upon local participation for the development of their plans. Funds are provided by a foundation for experiments and studies under the leadership of a recognized educational institution. The Extension Division has been able to participate in such arrangements. At present the Division is serving as the clearing house agency of a trust fund established by the Filene Good Will Fund, for an experiment in consumer cooperatives and credit unions among the negroes of the State.

The Commonwealth Fund desirous of promoting better understanding between the Americas gives financial assistance to the work of the Inter-American Institute.

The General Education Board, The Laura Spelman Rockefeller Foundation, The Office of the Coordinator of Inter-American Affairs, The Carnegie Foundation and The Rosenwald Fund are among the national agencies with which cooperative programs have been developed.

VI
UNIVERSITY AGENCIES OF ADULT EDUCATION

UNIVERSITY AGENCIES OF ADULT EDUCATION

The Bureau of Business Services and Research

REX WINSLOW, DIRECTOR

In November, 1945 the University Administration approved the establishment of a Bureau of Business Services and Research as an autonomous unit within the School of Commerce. The primary object of this Bureau is to enlist, coordinate, and extend available resources of the University to businesses and industries of the State.

This extension will take the form of research projects, special training classes, conferences and institutes, on the adult level; and consultant, informative, and publication services. The Extension Division will administer the training program, issue some of the publications, and coordinate the Bureau with other extension work.

Relations are necessarily so close that the operations office of the Bureau has been set up as an integral part of the administrative offices of the Extension Division. The Extension Division was instrumental in establishing the Bureau. It supported the proposal, aided in outlining Bureau functions, provided office equipment and clerical assistance, and absorbed some of the Bureau budget.

The rejuvination of this phase of University extension was stimulated by the mutual benefits flowing to North Carolina business and to the University from the war training program in production management administered by the Extension Division for the U. S. Office of Education. Future opportunities for the University to contribute through extension work to the business prosperity and economic well-being of the State are unlimited.

The Folklore Council

The Folklore Council has been quietly carrying on its work since 1935. Organized to perpetuate and disseminate all phases of folklore it has served as an educational agency in collecting, preserving and interpreting our national heritage of folk culture. The Council has recognized the variety of interest represented in folklore and has embraced the fields of art, English, drama, and music to secure a well balanced program.

The Council had its beginnings in the Institute of Folk Music which was organized in 1931. With the head of the Music Department serving as chairman the Institute developed a three-fold program divided as follows: 1. Research: discovering, collecting, and publishing native folk music; 2. Educational work: (a) teaching traditional songs and dances in schools and communities, (b) organizing county folk festivals and "old time music" conventions, (c) publishing English and American folk songs and folk dances for educational and social use in schools and communities; 3. Creative composition based on folk music.

Lamar Stringfield's well known composition "Cripple Creek" was produced as a result of his work with this project. The North Carolina Symphony Society which is now a thriving independent organization had its beginnings in the Institute of Folk Music, and the Dogwood Festival which brought together the folk arts of drama, handicraft, and music was an early activity of the Institute.

The Dogwood Festival focused attention upon the variety of interests in folklore represented by the members of the advisory board of the Institute. Each rightfully maintained that his interest be given more consideration. As a result the Folklore Council was organized to include all the cultural aspects of folk life and the Institute of Folk Music became a Division of that Council.

Since its organization in 1935 the Director of the Extension

Division has served as the Chairman of the Council. He has also served for four years as secretary and treasurer of the Southeastern Folklore Society and has cooperated with the programs of the National Folk Festival, thus carrying the interest of the University into national fields.

Through its membership the Council has made a number of valuable collections, many of which have been recorded and published.

The Music Department realizing the importance of trained workers in this field offers regular courses in folk music and comparative musicology.

THE INSTITUTE FOR RESEARCH IN SOCIAL SCIENCE

KATHERINE JOCHER, ASSISTANT DIRECTOR

The Institute for Research in Social Science, organized at the University of North Carolina in 1924, is one of the two permanent Institutes—the other being the Institute of Government—in the University. Following as it did the early beginnings of the Extension Division, the University of North Carolina Press, and particularly, under the leadership of Dr. E. C. Branson, the Department of Rural Social-Economics with its slogan of "Know your State," the Institute, under the able direction of Howard W. Odum and later of Gordon W. Blackwell, with Katharine Jocher as assistant director, followed closely this tradition and pattern of a primary function of a state university—that of serving its state. And moving on from this the Institute added, as another major function, service to the region.

Accordingly, even though primarily a research agency with grants specifically earmarked for research in the social sciences in North Carolina and the South, the Institute has always conceived of its function in a threefold manner. First, it has attempted to encourage and stimulate research in the social sciences at the University of North Carolina and throughout the South, to discover and develop research personnel, and to map out and plan for a program of coordinated and cooperative research in the southern regions, particularly the Southeast. Its second function grew naturally out of the first, namely, to become a training center for research and planning personnel and teachers especially within the region which the Institute primarily serves. In the third place, focusing as it does upon regional research, the Institute acts as a center for cooperating with other agencies in the field in an attempt not only to stimulate more adequate research but to develop procedures and techniques for interpreting this research and making it of more functional value in the State and region.

In addition to its numerous publications, many of which bear the imprint of the University of North Carolina Press, the Institute has from time to time sponsored, promoted, and conducted conferences and institutes in its effort to make available its findings, not only to individuals, but to agencies which might take its facts and figures and build from them a constructive program of social and economic development for the South.

One of the earliest of these was a Work Conference on Optimum Production with Special Reference to Selected Agriculture Commodities in the Southern Region, which was held on April 3, 1933. Morning and evening sessions were held in Alumni Building, the home of the Institute, with a special luncheon meeting at the Carolina Inn. The specific purpose of this conference was "to inquire into the availability of a study and planning project in optimum production as a field for special extended effort and as an approach to the study of planned and controlled regional production." Joining with the Institute in sponsoring the sessions were: The Southern Regional Committee of the Social Science Research Council; The Southern

Regional Study Work Group of the Southern Regional Study, the findings of which were published under the title of *Southern Regions of the United States*, by Howard W. Odum; and the Southern Tax Committee. The members of the Forestry and Research Committees of the Southeastern Council were also invited to attend and participate. Approximately eighty persons attended the sessions, which featured nationally known specialists together with University personnel, as speakers and discussion leaders.

However, it was an Institute on Southern Regional Development and the Social Sciences, held in Alumni Building, June 17-27, 1936, which actually took the first step toward the recently organized program of research interpretation of the Institute for Research in Social Science with John E. Ivey, Jr., as its head (See pp. 163-65). Among the several conditions which led to the decision to hold this Institute and which in large measure determined its nature and work, the following should be recorded:

1. The publication and wide discussion of *Southern Regions of the United States*, by Howard W. Odum, which led some of its sponsors to conclude that further consideration of its findings, a wider use through simplified presentation, and further consideration of actual planning in certain fields of regional economy and culture might be profitably discussed in such a conference.

2. An increasing interest in regionalism and regional planning, not only in the South but throughout the Nation, together with the need for more effective ways and means of utilizing the vast amount of research material which had been gathered by so many agencies.

3. An opportunity for cooperative stock-taking to discover the best uses which could be made of the materials which southern universities and colleges had been gathering and publishing for many years, together with developing extension teaching and research.

4. A consideration of the special conclusions which come from *Southern Regions* with reference to the reconstruction of southern agriculture, in order to bring about a better coordination of research and extension teaching among

the land-grant colleges and between the land-grant colleges and the universities.

5. The timeliness of a review of the whole prospect of regionwide coordination in research and social action, particularly in relation to recent meetings of southern groups.

Between fifty and sixty visiting specialists were in attendance at the conference. In addition, more than two score members of the University of North Carolina faculty took part. The institute was a working conference of university people, having for its purpose a sort of stock-taking to see what the universities, the colleges, and the professors could contribute to actual planning and development; what next steps in coordination of their work should be taken; and what, if any, future coordinating committees should be set up. It was expected that the findings of the institute would be made available later to all interested planning groups and agencies. The institute itself, however, was not a planning conference; first and last, it was a working body seeking testing fields for the use of research data in regional development. In addition to the *Review* and *Summary of Findings*, distributed in mimeographed form, the *Manual for Southern Regions of the United States*, by Lee M. Brooks and others, was largely an outgrowth of this institute.

Another major step in research, planning, and interpretation was achieved through a University Conference on Population Research, Regional Research, the Measurement of Regional Development, which was held April 30-May 4, 1940, with headquarters in the then newly remodeled Alumni Building. Since one of the major themes of the week was that of regional population study, it was peculiarly fortunate that the Population Association of America held its annual meeting at the same time and place, so that joint sessions could be planned. The conference was the result of a felt need, on the one hand, for a sort of stock-taking during the decade 1930-1940, and a look ahead toward the ten years from 1940 to 1950. Some of its objectives were stated in this light:

1. To explore the extent to which current social and economic inventories might show status and trends of southern regional development at the time of the conference.

2. To indicate to what extent the earlier southern regional study, as represented by *Southern Regions of the United States*, might be brought up to date and utilized as a measure of future trends and development.

3. To re-examine the field and methods of regional research and explore the possibilities of new ways of measuring regional development.

4. To explore more fully the nature and possibilities of the Subregional Laboratory for Social Research and Planning (an area of thirteen contiguous counties, approximating a miniature Piedmont South, with ten counties in North Carolina and three in Virginia, as an exploratory unit in social research and planning).

5. To examine the availability of social science exhibits in regional research and planning as effective illustrative materials. A special feature, therefore, was the exhibition representative of regionalism, both world and national, which had been prepared especially for the conference and which appeared on the walls of the Laboratory-Workshop of the Institute, in which all sessions were held.

6. To explore the extent to which new cooperative efforts in research and planning might be focused upon next steps both within specific laboratories and in the region at large.

7. To feature a unit of the University's Sesquicentennial activities and the remodeling of the Alumni Building as a center for the work of the Institute for Research in Social Science in cooperation with other social sciences and social work.

The membership of the conference necessarily was limited. However, all sessions were open and visiting students were welcome. Approximately one hundred persons attended one or more sessions. Flexibility in the program permitted the discussion of a wide variety of topics such as: southern population and population research; the general structure of southern regional industry; the southern climate and its effects; race and regional culture; attitudes, education, the library, the press, and civic efforts. There were no resolutions, no findings, and no recommendations, but it was hoped that out of this conference would come continuing exploration and inquiry leading to next steps in social research and planning.

Cooperating with the Institute of World Economics, the Institute sponsored a one-day working conference on Regionalism in World Economics, held on April 21, 1945. The conference was under the joint direction of Professor W. G. Friederick, of North Carolina State College of the University of North Carolina, and Gordon W. Blackwell, Director of the Institute for Research in Social Science. Morning and afternoon sessions were held in the Laboratory-Workshop of the Institute, 403 Alumni Building, with a luncheon conference at the Carolina Inn. Because of transportation restrictions only a limited number of out-of-town guests were invited, but all sessions were open to the general public. The papers and discussions, featuring national and local authorities, centered about the impact on the southern regions of present world happenings and included such topics as: the premises of regional balance; transportation factors and regional development; regional development projects abroad; public policy in regional economics; regionalism and geo-economics; regional industrialization and standards of living; regional development of American markets for imports; national aspects of regional development. Wall exhibits, prepared especially for the conference, and a table display of current books on regionalism and world economcis supplemented the formal papers and discussions.

A somewhat different type of conference, yet nonetheless educational and interpretive, was the Lecture-Seminar-Conference on the Education of the American Negroes and the African Natives, held for the purpose of bringing together a number of educators of wide experience from the United States and from the British territories in Africa to discuss the problems of the education of the American Negroes and of the Native Africans. The conference was conducted jointly by the University of North Carolina, Yale University, and Hampton Institute, with Howard W. Odum of the Institute for Research in Social Science and Charles T. Loram of Yale University, directors.

This Lecture-Seminar-Conference, held from September 1 to October 27, 1937, was attended by approximately sixty delegates. The members from the United States were, for the most part, the State Agents for Negro Education in the South, while the members from South Africa, selected by the British Colonial Office and the Government of the Union of South Africa, included educational officials in the service of the several British colonies and the Union of South Africa, together with some distinguished missionary educators.

The conference was divided into four periods. From September 1 to 29, the participants were at Chapel Hill for lectures, seminars, and discussions. From September 29 to October 31, the State Agents of Negro Education took the overseas visitors to see Negro schools in action. From October 13 to 20, the group met at Hampton Institute for the consideration of problems of agricultural, industrial, and normal school education. The last week of the meeting, from October 20-27, was spent at Yale University for additional lectures and for summarizing the conference.

While at Chapel Hill the delegates were accomodated at the Carolina Inn. The ball room equipped with table space for each member served as seminar headquarters. There were displays of pertinent publications furnished by the Yale University Press and the University of North Carolina Press. Motion pictures provided by the Museum of Art supplemented facts about this country, which limited travel time could not provide. An intense work period was covered each day with activities beginning at nine in the morning and ending at ten o'clock at night, with recesses for relaxation and socialization interspersed. The conference was considered of special value as a medium for international understanding.

Distinctly educational and contributing in a large measure to better living is the Annual Conference on Conservation of Marriage and the Family, which met first during the summer of 1934. It resulted from the interest of college teachers in the methodology of instruction in preparation for marriage that had been developed at the University of North Carolina. Although succeeding programs continued to feature discussions of the problems of teaching marriage, they also included other topics relating to the conservation of marriage and the family and were broader in their appeal. This was in accord with the interests developed by the preceding conferences. For example, the ninth conference, which held its sessions, April 9-11, 1946, emphasized marriage counseling with a program on the third day under the auspices of the American Association of Marriage Counselors. The conference has always been under the direction of its founder, Ernest R. Groves, research professor in the Institute for Research in Social Science. In earlier years, Duke University cooperated with the University of North Carolina in sponsoring the conference, with one or more sessions being held on the Duke campus. Now the conference has been taken over entirely by the University of North Carolina.

The programs have always been made up of co-laborers in the field of marriage and the family engaged in practical services, teaching, or scientific investigation, and have featured national authorities in the several fields. In order to maintain its purpose—the meeting of specialists for discussion of common problems—the conference has not been open to the general public. In order also to maintain the intimate character of the conference and provide the best conditions for discussion, attendance has been limited to about one hundred and fifty persons. Invitations are so distributed as to permit representation from a wide geographical area and the recognition of many different backgrounds of interest. Members have come from as far west as California and as far north as Canada.

At its closing business session, the Ninth Conference went on record that the conference be continued, with annual meetings at Chapel Hill, under the direction of Professor Groves with Gladys Hoagland Groves as co-director and Ray V. Sowers as associate director.

These major conferences and institutes are but milestones on the road of research and planning for which the Institute has broken the ground and along which it continues to move, clearing new paths, year by year. In between, there have been smaller meetings of committees and groups in many ways of equal importance since they have often shown the need and pointed the way to next steps for the more formal discussions. And now, added impetus and stimulation will be given to this essential phase of the threefold function of the program of the Institute for Research in Social Science through the coordinating and interpreting services of its Division of Research Interpretation which is already well on the way to serving the State and the region.

The Institute of Government

Albert Coates, Director

The Institute of Government unites public officials, private citizens, and students and teachers of civics and government, in a systematic effort to meet definite and practical needs in North Carolina.

Aims and Objectives

1. *To bridge the gap between government as it is taught in*

the schools and as it is practiced in the city halls, county courthouses, and the state capitol.

This need grows out of the fact that, with rare exceptions, the high schools, colleges, and professional schools of North Carolina are each year graduating around 20,000 boys and girls who know something of textbook civics but little of practical government; know how to read a page of Latin but are unable to read their own municipal balance sheet; know how to find their way around Rome but not how to find their way around their own city hall, county courthouse, or state capitol. As a result thousands of officials are going into office without an opportunity to acquaint themselves with their powers and duties or the methods and practices of their predecessors. Hundreds of thousands of citizens are going to the ballot box without adequate understanding of the workings of their governmental institutions.

2. *To provide the machinery for putting the people in touch with their government and keeping them in touch with it.*

This need grows out of the fact that citizens for the most part do not become acquainted with the practical workings of their government in high school and college classrooms; that after they leave school they do not have any systematic way of keeping in touch with it as they busy themselves with the varied tasks of making a living; that in times of stress and strain they try to cut the climbing costs of government by organizing taxpayers' leagues and citizens' committees; that these leagues and committees are ill-equipped to find the facts they need to know; that even when they find the facts in their own local units they are crippled by the lack of a clearing house for the exchange of comparative governmental information with other units. These feverish organizations come and go with every depression. They have once more largely disappeared; but they lived long enough to point out with all the stinging freshness of demonstrated truth that foresight costs less than hindsight, that citizens can be constant sources of help instead of hindrance to their officials, and can save thousands of dollars for themselves by attending to their government as they attend to their business.

3. *To co-ordinate governmental machinery in overlapping governmental units and eliminate useless friction and waste.*

This need grows out of the fact that in the last 150 years the people of North Carolina have built on one land a pyramid of overlapping governmental units—federal, state, county, township, town, and special district. This means that a person committing a crime within city limits may be subject to arrest by city police, county sheriff, state patrol, or federal agent; that he may be prosecuted by a city, county, state, or federal prosecuting attorney; sentenced by a city, county, state, or federal judge; and sent to a city, county, state, or federal prison. It means that taxes may be levied and collected from the same citizens by city, county, state, and federal agencies. It means that we live under pyramiding laws enacted by city councilmen, county commissioners, state legislators, and federal representatives. For 150 years city, county, state, and federal officials have been working on the same problems for the same people in overlapping and adjoining governmental units without coming together in the practice of co-ordinated effort.

4. *To bridge the gap in knowledge and experience between outgoing and incoming public officials and cut down the lost time, lost motion, and lost money involved in a rotating governmental personnel.*

This need grows out of the fact that we are committed to the theory and practice of elective officers, short terms in office, and rotation of officers. This means that every two years hosts of newly elected officials take office in the cities, the counties, and the State of North Carolina—too often knowing very little about the powers, duties, and administration of their offices—learning as they go. When their terms end, they are replaced by others who pick up the threads of administration, not where their predecessors left off, but almost if not quite where they began. Popular government, like the frog in the well, goes forward three feet and falls back two. Accumulated governmental knowledge goes over the wheel to waste. Government is forever in the hands of beginners who do not always have beginners' luck. This is costly training for which the people pay—not in the beginning but in the end. Private business, operating in this fashion, would go broke before beginners learned their business. Public business likewise may go broke before beginners learn their government.

More than common honesty is required in public office and likewise more than common sense. A hundred thousand dollars lost through honest inefficiency is as great a burden to the taxpayer as a hundred dollars lost through conscious fraud. Knowledge is no guarantee of character, we are told. Neither is ignorance. The best of governmental systems may be wrecked by men who do not understand it. After 200 years in the building of governmental machinery, we are beginning the training of the men who run it.

5. *To build a demonstration laboratory and clearing house of governmental information.*

This need grows out of the fact that while business men have been building their laboratories to analyze and compare the business methods and practices of others in order to improve their own, after 200 years of local self-government in North Carolina public officials have yet to build a governmental demonstration laboratory and clearing house of methods and practices in government.

The value of such a laboratory is illustrated by the following:

a. Improved practices of one tax supervisor in one year added 4,000 new taxpayers and $5,000,000 in newly discovered property to the tax books to lighten the load on those already there.
b. One city reorganized its tax collecting machinery, improved its operations and cut down the cost of operation $6,500 annually.
c. The accounting system of one governmental agency was simplified and the cost of annual audits reduced from $1,800 to $300.
d. One local official saved the cost of his salary by improved methods in the administration of his office.
e. At least one local unit has worked out methods by which 98% of its taxes are collected in the current year while methods of some other units collect around 50%.

When specific illustrations such as these may be multiplied over and over again and new methods, worth their weight in gold, are continually arising out of the initiative and resourcefulness of public officials, the rewards of lifting the poorest governmental practices to the level of the best begin to dawn upon us, and the importance of this demonstration laboratory and clearing house of information is apparent.

Sources of Information—Comparative Studies of Laws and Practices

A small percentage of our governmental knowledge is in the books—scattered through constitutions, statutes, decisions, and administrative rulings. The greater part is in the methods, practices, and experience of officials in 100 counties, 300 cities and towns, and four score or more state departments and agencies. The members of the staff of the Institute are now going from city to city, county to county, state department to state department, collecting, comparing, and classifying these laws and practices in books and in action.

The results of these comparative studies are being set forth in guidebooks, programs, and supplementary texts, taught in institutes, demonstrated in laboratories, and transmitted through the clearing house of information to the officials, the citizens, and the students and teachers of civics and government in the cities, the counties, and the State of North Carolina.

1. *Guidebooks, Programs, and Texts*

Set forth in guidebooks for officials, programs for citizens, texts for students and teachers of civics and government.

a. The *guidebooks* will bring to incoming officials in the cities, the counties, and the State clear and concise statements of the powers and duties of their offices, the methods and practices of their predecessors and of other officials in this and other states and thus help incoming officials pick up the threads of government nearer the point where their predecessors left off than where they began.

b. The *programs for governmental study and discussion* will bring to citizens throughout the State clear, concise, and accurate information about the structure and the workings of their state and local governmental institutions and thus help to put them in touch with their government and keep them in touch with it. Materials for these purposes, prepared and published by' The Institute of Government during the last three years, include 150 studies and articles adding up to 1800 printed pages.

2. *Institutes*

Taught in institutes for officials, citizens, students, and teachers of civics and government.

a. *Institutes for officials* will bring together city, county, state, and federal officials in systematic study of their common problems and lay the basis for co-ordinating governmental machinery in overlapping governmental units.

b. *Institutes for public affairs committees of civic organizations* of men and women will acquaint them with current developments in state and local governments, and enable them to turn the public affairs meetings in their respective organizations into a systematic program of governmental education throughout the year on a local and statewide scale.

c. *Institutes for students and teachers of civics and government in the schools* will equip them to interpret the current developments in government and its administration and focus them in the classroom at the classroom hour.

3. *Governmental Laboratory*

Demonstrated in governmental laboratory offices to which successive generations of officials, citizens, students, and teachers of civics and government may go to see illustrated in one place the methods and practices in use in city halls, county courthouses, and state departments throughout North Carolina.

4. *Clearing House of Information*

Transmitted through the clearing house of governmental information to city halls, county courthouses, state departments, federal agencies, the schoolrooms and the people; between local units, between state and local units, between federal, state, and local units; and between officials, citizens, and students and teachers of government.

The Inter-American Institute
Sturgis E. Leavitt, Director

The University of North Carolina has long been interested in Latin America. Members of the faculty have been engaged in research in the Hispanic-American field, the university has been developing a collection of Latin American materials, and its curriculum has touched upon Latin America in various ways. There were many reasons, therefore, for it to be selected in 1940 to conduct an experiment which was destined to be far reaching in its results.

In 1940 the Institute of International Education, the Grace Steamship Line, and the Pan American Union approached the University of North Carolina with the suggestion that it act as host to a group of students and professional people to be brought from South America during their vacation months to attend a special session similar to the usual summer schools for North Americans held in Latin America.

The suggestion met with favor and a sponsoring group was formed to coordinate the interests and activities already established at the University of North Carolina and to carry out the summer school idea. Thus it was that the Inter-American Institute of the University of North Carolina was established. Sturgis E. Leavitt was appointed Director, and J. C. Lyons, Executive Secretary. An advisory committee and a working committee were appointed. Steamship companies, the Institute of International Education, the Carnegie Endowment for International Peace, the American Council of Learned Societies, the Office of the Coordinator of Inter-American Affairs, and the Pan American Union, all gave their support to the undertaking.

The program of instruction for the "Winter Summer School," so-called because it was held in the South American summer months of January, February and March, aimed to provide for the individual interests of the students and to present to them characteristic aspects of life in the United States. Practically all the departments of the University cooperated in the effort, and the usual university activities were supplemented by additional lectures, trips to other educational centers and industrial plants, radio broadcasts, social functions, and many other first-hand contacts with the "Average American." One hundred and eight students and professional people attended, representing seven countries from South America. Thirty-seven were women, and seventy-one were men.

The lack of an adequate command of English on the part of a number of the group created considerable difficulty. To aid in solving this problem I. A. Richards, Head of the Orthological Institute in Cambridge, Mass., offered his services, and he and his staff were most successful with instruction in Basic English. The problems of individual interests in professional work were met by the cooperation of the staff of the Duke University Medical School, the faculty of State College, the military personnel at Fort Bragg, and others. The departments of the University held individual conferences with those having special problems.

The Extension Division served as the business agent for the school. It was responsible for much of the correspondence, publicity, details of financing, and business agreements with transportation companies, hotels, and publishing houses.

The 1941 "Winter Summer School" was generally considered a definite contribution to the Good Neighbor Policy. A second school was planned for 1942, and lessons learned from the first experiment were expected to improve the selection of students, the daily schedule, and the program in general. Registrations were promising and a large number of students seemed assured when Pearl Harbor and consequent dangers of ocean travel threatened to cancel out all the plans. However, eleven students from three countries attended. The aims of the 1942 school remained the same, but the methods were adjusted to meet the needs of a smaller number of students. For a fuller statement of how these schools operated and what they accomplished the reader is referred to mimeographed reports prepared by the Director.

The two special sessions of "Winter Summer School" just described were a spectacular demonstration of the great interest in Latin America felt by the University of North Carolina; but on account of war conditions, it seemed for a time that further activities would have to be postponed. It was therefore a happy surprise to be asked by the U. S. Office of Education and the State Department to cooperate in a session for Mexican teachers who were being brought to the United States to improve their knowledge of English and to observe methods of instruction.

A party of five men and five women arrived in January, 1943, and stayed in Chapel Hill until the last of February. All were teachers of English in Mexico City and for them classes were organized in Public Speaking, Diction, Phonetics, Conversation, and Methods of Instruction. Each class was directed by a specialist, and individual improvement was most satisfactory. Academic training was supplemented by life in dormitories and private homes, by student entertainments, athletic events, attendance at moving picture theaters, and informal parties given by local residents. A trip to Raleigh during which the students met the Governor and were entertained by Mr. and Mrs. Josephus Daniels was the high light of their stay.

As on previous occasions, the Extension Division played an important part in making this school possible. Assuming responsibility for business matters, it made arrangements for housing, transportation, trips, and incidentals necessary to physical comfort.

In 1944 the Division of Education of the Commonwealth Fund worked out a plan whereby an English school was to be conducted for Commonwealth Fellows to be brought from Latin America to study medicine in the United States. The experience gained from previous schools gave the University an unusual opportunity for service on this occasion. The Fellows in attendance were professionally trained as doctors or engineers.

They came to Chapel Hill with the express purpose of increasing their ability to understand English and to learn to express themselves in this difficult language in order to profit from study in their professional fields.

For this school the mornings were devoted to class instruction. Sometimes the students met as a unit and at other times in small groups, as the need dictated. Definite attention was given to increasing vocabulary and to improving diction. The afternoons were spent in small groups observing work of a typical North American university, and some time was devoted to the acquisition of a scientific vocabulary. Lectures were given in the evening to provide training in understanding connected discourse. Moving pictures proved a source of both entertainment and instruction. Passes were issued by the local management to all members of the group and many students attended with the regularity of a class assignment. From time to time question periods followed attendance at the movies in order to ascertain how much the students understood. This school was attended by ten doctors and two engineers. Nine countries were represented.

A second school for Latin American doctors was sponsored by the Commonwealth Fund in 1945, with highly satisfactory results. This school was attended by ten doctors of medicine and one pharmacist. Eight countries were represented.

The University of North Carolina Press

Thomas J. Wilson, Director

An article on The University of North Carolina Press in a book on the University's Extension Division might seem at first blush to be an anomaly. The responsibility of the Extension Division is to spread the teaching, and the cultural and economic benefits and influence, of the University beyond the geographical limits of the campus. The function of the Press is obviously to produce books for public consumption. But, on further consideration, the essentially close relationship between these two parts of the University becomes clear. For the publication of books to be read by the people is after all just another way of "extending" the University's services beyond the local classrooms. It falls in the same category and is on the same level of importance, to my mind, as the Extension Division's Communication Center, its correspondence courses, its lectures in the farthest corners of the State, and its seminars, conferences, and general meetings here at Chapel Hill.

Various tangible evidences symbolize the kinship of the Extension Division and the Press, and the mutuality of their fundamental interests. The Director of the Extension Division is a member of the Board of Governors of the Press and of that board's Finance Committee. Other Governors of the Press are active in the affairs of the Extension Division. The *Extension Bulletin,* now in its 25th volume, is prepared and distributed by the Extension Division, but is published under the imprint of The University of North Carolina Press and is one of those regular periodical publications on the Press list which have contributed heavily to the reputation of the Press in the public eye. Other direct connections and relationships between these two parts of the University could be brought forward. They do not appear necessary, however; the actual and tangible interlocking of the Extension Division and the Press, important as it may be, is not the reason for the presence of an article about the Press in this book; nor do the evidences of such an interlocking stand as more than a mere sign of the work of the Press in extension.

The books of the Press, and its periodical publications *other* than those for which the Extension Division is primarily responsible, constitute the real service of the Press in bringing the

University into the homes and the lives of the people of the State and the region. These book and magazine publications, with no apparent connection with the Extension Division, are in themselves independent and informal instruments in extending the service of the University of North Carolina. Governed by no course of study, and having as subject any chosen field of human knowledge, interest, or endeavor, each of these works acts as a missionary of the University to readers everywhere; together they form a fruitful and diverse source-book of learning, entertainment, and practical information which is as truly a part of the offering of a modern university as its classes on the campus.

The University of North Carolina Press was founded in 1922, under the directorship of Dr. Louis R. Wilson and with a Board of Governors composed of those faculty members and alumni who, perhaps better than others, understood the full potential of the University as a servant of the State and the region and as a force for growth and improvement. Under Dr. Wilson's guidance until 1932, and then, after his resignation, under the directorship of Mr. W. T. Couch, the Press has weathered many threatening storms, has faced actual bankruptcy more than once, but has continued to grow in the volume and, more important, in the quality of its offerings until today it stands in the very forefront of the university presses of the nation. Still far from being the largest academic publishing concern, still faced with real financial problems and unable because of them to contribute its maximum to the welfare of its public, the Press is recognized as the most important publishing house in the South and, to a large extent, as the true voice of the region. On its list stand works of authors from every corner of this country and from many foreign countries; its books are sold wherever books in English can be read and American goods purchased. This diversity of authorship and this breadth of distribution are of course marks of the distinction of the Press. But, in the final analysis, the books by North Carolina and southern authors for regional consumption constitute the major work of the Press "in extension" and are at the same time the foundation of its greatness as an enlightener of the people it serves. Proud as the Press may be of its "foreign" books and authors, its contribution in the long run will be measured in terms of the value to the South of the works it publishes by native and adopted sons and daughters of the South—works by writers who may be called Odum, Vance, Johnson, Paul Green, Koch, Couch, Coulter, Bullock, Sharpe, Coker, Waterman, Harris, or Daniels—or whose names may be entirely new but yet akin to those names in the tradition of service. The primary purpose of the Press is to advance the learning and to increase the material and spiritual welfare of North Carolina and the South. The published work by which it will continue to accomplish that purpose will be the work of those who know the South, love it for its virtues, and are determined to eliminate its vices.

Today the University of North Carolina Press stands at a crossroad. After seeing the Press through its childhood and adolescence and marking its attainment of maturity, Mr. W. T. Couch resigned the directorship in the Fall of 1945 to become Director of the University of Chicago Press. To a large extent W. T. Couch *was* The University of North Carolina Press for twelve years or more. He took the responsibility for the books it published; he saw that these books had a fair chance to reach their intended or putative markets; he pinched pennies and saved dollars to make both ends meet when less courageous men would have concluded that the State would not or could not give him the support he had to have. When he left the Press, it had achieved the dignity and continuity of a full-fledged publishing concern; its annual lists averaged twenty-five or more volumes a year; its books, scholarly or popular, fell in fields ranging from higher mathematics and philosophy, through the natural and social sciences and the humanities, to fiction and poetry. With a Board of Governors made up of some of the ablest and most active members of the University faculty and with a staff of twenty trained employees, it was fully prepared to judge, to publish, and to promote the sale of any good book which came to its hands. And with a subsidy from the State, through the University, which had finally attained reasonably generous proportions, it could feel at least relatively secure, at least fairly confident that it would be able to continue its work and to grow in influence and service.

The staff of the Press and its present, newly-elected director are naturally determined to follow in the tradition of Louis R. Wilson and W. T. Couch and to extend the usefulness of the Press along and beyond the lines laid down by those two pioneers. Works of political, economic, and social analysis, works of history and science, works of creative genius in the fields of pure literature and the arts will be published as they come to the Press and as its funds permit. It will attempt to give just and fair consideration to every manuscript or book idea calculated to add to the learning of our people, or to their wealth, or to their enjoyment. Thus it may hope to fulfill its function of service to the people of the State and the South, and to *extend*, in the real sense of that word, the work of the University of which it is a component part.

VII
UNIVERSITY EXTENSION IN WARTIME

UNIVERSITY EXTENSION IN WARTIME

The pattern of University Extension during the war emergency (1941-1945), was quite similar to that during 1917-1918. In each of these war periods, the University made major adjustments to serve the nation. Extension services were likewise adjusted to meet the needs of the time.

During World War I, the Bureau of Extension was very active in publishing and distributing literature, in sending lecturers to communities throughout the State, and in other ways guiding the wartime thinking of North Carolinians.

World War II, because of its scope and duration, caused many more adjustments to be necessary. The induction into the service of essential personnel at a time when activities were increasing was only one of the many administrative problems growing out of the emergency. The University Administration in its attempt to house adequately the Navy and Army Units installed here, found it necessary to move the Extension Division offices several times. Each time there was a telescoping effect, making efficient work more and more difficult. Thus, short-staffed and in cramped quarters, the assuming of war demands necessitated adjustments of finances, personnel, time, and equipment. How successfully this adjustment was made may be judged by the following account of activities.

The heads of bureaus and services of the Extension Division found that the war presented new challenges. While keeping alive essential activities already in the annual calendar, they shifted the emphasis in work, added new ideas, and produced programs aimed at meeting these new demands. In most cases the war heightened interest and vitalized existing procedures. The volume of work increased considerably in most of these departments.

Adjustment of Existing Activities

THE CAROLINA DRAMATIC ASSOCIATION

Each year during the war, spring gave rise to the same question as to the advisability of holding a Drama Festival. Each year the decision was the same, the Festival was held. It brought to "the Hill" a surprising number who believed they should continue because of the war rather than in spite of it. The Association sincerely believed that the theater was playing a great role in the preservation of creative instincts during a period of destruction. To foster this idea, a new contest in playwriting was established for servicemen. This contest had specific rules for entry, stipulations for submitting manuscripts, arrangements for awards, and provision for the production of the winning play by the Carolina Playmakers. Two such plays were produced by the Playmakers. One was published commercially. The continuance of activities and the broadening of policies kept the Association in a position to meet the challenge presented by the war.

THE CAROLINA PLAYMAKERS

In the early days of the war, the National Theater Conference was asked by the United States Army to sponsor a theater experiment in an army camp. This assignment fell to the Carolina Playmakers. Under the direction of "Proff" Koch, Joseph Lee Brown went to Fort Bragg and organized a "little theater" program for the camp. It was an experiment in army life, but its success was confirmed by the fact that later when the Army organized the Special Services Corps, the fundamental ideas and plans developed by Mr. Brown were incorporated in its program.

Tours carrying Playmaker productions to all parts of the State have for years been part of the annual schedule. These were continued and expanded to include U.S.O. clubs and military installations. The playbill was made to fit the occasion. Camp productions, put on in the lighter vein, were double-duty shock absorbers, furnishing fun and frolic for both the actors and the audience.

THE CAROLINA INSTITUTE OF INTERNATIONAL RELATIONS

This organization has, from its inception, been dedicated to the idea of "creating a better understanding of world affairs." Its programs have always stressed the interpretation of economic and social conditions affecting world peace. After Pearl Harbor, more emphasis was put upon the part the United States must play in world reconstruction. Discussions placed responsibility upon this nation for world organization, education, religion, and economic security, challenging all intelligent leaders to interpret this responsibility to the people.

Due to the shortage of accommodations, the summer institute, which had for many years been held on the Chapel Hill campus, was transfered to the Woman's College at Greensboro. During the war years a growing interest in world affairs was indicated by the large increase in the number of people attending the Carolina Institute on International Relations.

FILM SERVICE

The Bureau of Visual Instruction, through its rental library, has for years been furnishing schools and civic groups with films and slides for educational purposes. With the advent of war and its accompanying problems, many new films were needed. The Office of War Information used the University Film Library as a depository for its informational films. These were listed in a special supplement of the Audio-Visual Aids Catalogue and were widely distributed throughout the State.

Other agencies following the same policy were: the British Office of War Information, the United States Department of Agriculture, the Office of the Coordinator of Inter-American Affairs, the Canadian Film Service, and the French Film Service. Such titles as "Black Market," "Mission Accomplished," "She Serves Abroad," "Food for Combat," and "The Fighting French Navy," helped to interpret war emergencies to the general public.

HIGH SCHOOL DEBATING

Little change was necessary in the general procedures of this activity to make it serve war needs. Recognizing the opportunity to provide free discussion of questions growing out of the conflict, the attention of the schools and the public was focused on such questions as "Post-War Organization for World Peace" and "Compulsory Military Training." Travel difficulties and the lack of adequate housing facilities made it necessary to limit the number of contestants coming to Chapel Hill. This fact necessitated a change in the method of conducting the preliminary contests. The adjustments made served wartime conditions but are not recommended as a permanent arrangement.

RADIO PROGRAMS

The physical facilities for radio were definitely curtailed by the changes brought about on the campus due to the war. For more than two years, the equipment was stored in packing boxes, scattered over the campus. It was moved intermittently as the demand for more space increased. Each move resulted in breakage and loss. When at last space was found, it was impossible to secure replacements of essential parts. Despite these difficulties, broadcasts were resumed. The emphasis was placed on discussion and forums that would aid in the understanding of national problems created by war. The Department of Journalism and interested faculty members participated. Music and drama returned to their usual roles on the air.

THE SOUTHERN COUNCIL ON INTERNATIONAL RELATIONS

The war quickened interest in world affairs. People became map conscious, economic minded, and sincerely concerned about peoples in remote parts of the globe. Using these expanded interests as a spring board, the Southern Council on International Relations, working in close cooperation with the Extension Division, increased its membership and enlarged its program of adult education. The council furnished literature on current international affairs, arranged radio broadcasts, art exhibitions, open forums, lectures, and motion picture showings. It made press releases available and provided a loan service of books and pamphlets. The council also directed the North Carolina Lecture-Institute program of the Office of the Coordinator of Inter-American Affairs. Such lecturers as Hubert Herring and Guy Inman toured the State carrying first-hand information to local communities.

NEW ACTIVITIES

Many of the problems growing out of war conditions could obviously not be met through existing educational agencies. It became necessary to develop additional services and activities. New Federal organizations were established and most of the old agencies initiated projects to aid the war effort. Several of these turned to the University for cooperation in carrying out their plans in North Carolina. The Extension Division representing the University, adjusted staff, finances and space whenever possible in order to expedite the wartime program of adult education.

UNIVERSITY CENTER FOR CIVILIAN MORALE SERVICE

Prior to Pearl Harbor, the United States Office of Education began a national program to bring about "intelligent and alert presentation and discussion of all issues concerning the war." The mechanism established for this achievement was known as The School and College Civilian Morale Service. The Director of the Extension Division became a member of the National Advisory Committee, and the University became a cooperating institution.

The Director of the Extension Division served as coordinator of the University's Center for Civilian Morale Service. Its work was divided among eight committees: library of information; public relations; curriculum studies; finance; forums, radio, institutes, and round tables; leadership training; research and preparation of materials; and publications.

Each of these committees, headed by a University faculty member well qualified for the responsibility, developed activities in their assigned field. Under the direction of Charles E. Rush, University Librarian, the Information Center at the Library assembled a "pertinent collection of books, pamphlets, reports, bibliographies, government publications, discussion outlines, and other up-to-the-minute materials." These materials were loaned without charge to individuals and organizations throughout the State.

The committee for research and preparation of materials constantly culled new publications for usable facts and ideas. These were arranged in suitable form for distribution to forum and discussion groups. Such groups increased in number, through the effort of the director of that division. Materials in packet form were furnished upon request. Forum speakers from the faculty and the student body were made available. The training of these student leaders was one of the functions of the Center. Radio played an important part in presenting the pros and cons of many questions. Regularly scheduled broadcasts featured round-table discussions of timely problems.

In providing these services to the State, the University had the cooperation of the State Department of Public Instruction, the State Council of National Defense, the State Library Commission, the N. C. College Conference, and many local groups representing the American Legion, P.T.A., civic clubs, labor unions, and negro groups.

ENGINEERING, SCIENCE, AND MANAGEMENT WAR TRAINING

Born of the pre-war shortage of engineers in war industries and christened as a Defense Training Program, the Engineering, Science, and Management War Training Program developed into a major activity lasting over a five-year period.

The program which was financed through the U. S. Office of Education was provided to "assist private industry with war contracts in selecting, recruiting, and training the additional manpower needed for all-out war production."

The Director of Extension was appointed a member of the National Advisory Committee and served also as "Institutional Representative" for the University. The Extension Division became headquarters for this work and a Field Representative was added to the staff. Thirteen teaching centers were established throughout the State. Instructors were sent out from the University, and others were selected from the local industries. As requests came in, courses were set up and approved so that industrial personnel shortages could be met locally as they arose. The program actually got underway in the fall of 1941. That year thirteen courses were taught in five centers. There was an enrollment of 395 students. Two hundred and twenty-one completed the work satisfactorily and were issued certificates. The work continued through the Spring of 1945. In all, a total of one thousand four hundred and seventy-eight students enrolled in the fifty-two courses offered. The subjects taught were: Manufacturing Accounting, Personnel Management, Production Cost Accounting, Fundamentals of Purchasing, Statistical Methods Applied to Quality Control, Physics for high school teachers, Industrial Management and Supervision, Physics for college teachers, Chemistry of Water Purification, and Time and Motion Study. Two courses were offered by correspondence, namely, Mathematics and Physics.

After V-E Day when changes were beginning to be made in many Federal agencies, the E.S.M.W.T. program was tapered off and discontinued on June 30, 1945.

UNITED STATES ARMED FORCES INSTITUTE

On April 22, 1942, the University of North Carolina signed a contract with the War Department to offer through the Army Institute (later changed to the United States Armed Forces Institute) certain correspondence courses to enlisted persons who had been in active service not less than four months, the Government paying one-half the cost of texts and tuition fees not to exceed $20.00 for any one course. Seventy-seven courses were approved, representing the departments of Economics and Commerce, Education, English, Geology and Geography, Sociology, and Rural Social-Economics. Later, courses in the departments of Art, Dramatic Art, and Philosophy were added and the contract was changed so that persons eligible to enroll through the Institute included enlisted persons who had been in the U. S. Army four months and personnel of the U. S. Navy, U. S. Coast Guard, and U. S. Marine Corps who had been in active service not less than two months. To date nearly one thousand servicemen and women have enrolled through the Institute. It is amazing, but encouraging, to find persons located in remote places all over the world, often threatened by attack or preparing to enter battle, eagerly trying to carry on their education. Among those endeavoring to continue their studies under what must have been extremely trying circumstances were men aboard numerous war ships, landing craft, coast guard cutters, in camps all over the United States and in the following distant places: North Africa, Italy, England, India, New Guinea, New Caledonia, Puerto Rico, South America, Guatemala, Panama, Alaska, and Hawaii. A staff sergeant in the Signal Corps wrote that he was on Martha's Vineyard Island for the purpose of carrying on certain tests. He stated that he worked all of the daylight hours of the day, seven days a week, and that he had to study by candlelight. He explained that he lived in a tent and that the weather was so cold that he found it necessary to go to bed early, so could not study at that particular time but intended going ahead with his work as soon as he could. The following was taken from a letter from a private first class: "I've written from ships, fox-holes, trenches, and other unusual places and under highly unusual circumstances. I've written on every type of paper imaginable. In fact, I am fortunate that I haven't had to use the actual bark from the trees. So my paper and materials will not always conform with the prescribed requirements." Much interest is shown in correspondence courses as evidenced by the large number of requests for information received from individuals and special service officers or educational directors. An average of six requests have been received daily for information about the correspondence courses offered through the Institute. Many officers in the Army who were ineligible to enroll through the Institute expressed their willingness to pay the fees themselves in order to continue their education. In such cases the usual registration fee of two dollars was waived and only in-state course fees were charged.

The United States Armed Forces Institute purchased, on a cost basis, for the use of army personnel overseas who were not interested in degree credit, copies of a two semester hour course in English, "Introduction to the Short Story," copies of a two semester hour course in Business English, copies of a three and one-third semester hour course in the same subject, copies of a course in Business Law, and copies of a more advanced course in the same subject. This material was printed, bound, packed, and shipped from Chapel Hill.

At the request and with the approval of the War Department correspondence courses were offered to enemy prisoners of war in this country. Course material was also sent to the War Prisoners' Aid of the YMCA to be forwarded to American prisoners in Germany, one of whom was a former University student.

Correspondence courses have been revised, when necessary, so as to confine required supplementary reading to books that are sold when the student enrolls or that may be made readily available to students not having access to good libraries.

The Director of Extension was recently appointed a member of the War-Navy Committee on the U. S. Armed Forces Institute.

CONFERENCES AND INSTITUTES

War emergencies necessitated the placing of many controls upon civilian activities. The success or failure of such controls depended to a large extent upon the intelligent cooperation of all those affected. To attain better understanding of certain government programs the University cooperated with governmental agencies in sponsoring conferences and institutes, the purpose of which was to interpret and clarify the civilians' part in a wartime economy.

Before Pearl Harbor, the Extension Division cooperated with the Workers' Education Bureau of America and the North Carolina Federation of Labor in sponsoring an Institute on "Labor in National Defense." At this time, representatives of labor and industry discussed the "Rights and Responsibilities" of each. The interdependence of labor and the farmer was developed and the relation of Government to labor explained. Speakers represented diversified groups so that well balanced discussions were possible.

After the war began, problems of interpretation developed rapidly. Because labor was affected both as a producer and a consumer, members of that group were particularly confused and at the same time their numbers made cooperation most important. The War Production Board, the Treasury Department, the Office of Price Administration, and the Office of Civilian Defense united in their efforts to explain the programs of their agencies. On the other hand, the American Federation of Labor, the Congress of Industrial Organizations, and the Standard Railway Brotherhoods united in an effort to understand the workings of these programs.

A Tri-State Conference on "Labor in the War" was held in the spring of 1942. Representatives from each governmental agency had a place on the program. Local labor unions in Virginia, South Carolina and North Carolina sent representatives. Attendance at the three-day meeting totaled three hundred and fifty.

With pressures continuing to mount, labor again sought clarification of national problems. It took the initiative and, probably for the first time in the history of organized labor, held a conference at which no discussion of labor problems, as such, took place. The sole purpose of the conference was to secure a better understanding of the controls placed upon citizens by the Office of Price Administration. The O.P.A. welcomed this opportunity to help educate the consumer in the principles of rationing. An institute on "How Labor Can Help Safeguard America's Wage Dollar" was held at the University in April 1944. Officials of the O.P.A. explained reasons for price control, rent control, and rationing. The aims of the program, the reasons for it, and suggestions for cooperation were clearly presented. Labor in North Carolina thus became more intelligently informed. Chester Bowles, Administrator of the Office of Price Administration, made this statment in writing to the group: "The success of the O.P.A. price and rationing program is determined by the extent to which the great mass of people in each community accept it as their own and work actively in support of it. Organized labor recognized this simple fact almost two years ago and since then has contributed more to the success of our program than any other organized consumer group."

Another conference for the purpose of interpreting the O. P. A. program was held in April 1945. At a "Symposium on the Consumer in Wartime," representatives of many consumer groups discussed the effect of price controls. Bankers, food dealers, clothing merchants, and consumers became more clearly aware of each other's problems. Officials of the government and representative citizens discussed their problems frankly together and the results were mutually beneficial.

COOPERATION WITH ARMY UNITS

From the very beginning of the draft, the Army provided educational opportunities for its personnel. Many of these were organized and supervised by the Army. Others were the result of cooperation between the Army and nearby educational institutions. The University of North Carolina was fortunate in being selected for such cooperation, and the Extension Division, in several instances, served as the coordinating agency.

One such service that provided much satisfaction has already been discussed under U.S.A.F.I. This provided a formal type of training leading to a degree. On the other hand, music, films, and lectures provided informal education and recreation. Since the return of wounded veterans to Army hospitals, this service has increased considerably. In cooperation with education and information officers, the Director of Extension undertook to provide lecturers who could interpret history and discuss economic, social, and political problems in a popular manner to audiences varying widely in intelligence and educational background.

The University Film Library was used extensively by nearby camps. To aid in the selection of titles, the Bureau of Audio-Visual Education issued a special supplement to its regular catalogue. Many films have been used for orientation, appreciation of national resources, and cultural backgrounds, as well as for entertainment. Convalescent hospitals were heavy users of these films.

Prisoner of War Camps located in North Carolina were also served. Correspondence courses were made available so that prisoners could continue their studies. Albums of classical music, films, and lecture services were used to a limited extent. One lecturer from the University, who was born in Germany and later became an American citizen, spoke very successfully before an audience of 1200 prisoners. He was asked to return several times and, according to American officers in charge, his contribution to straight thinking can hardly be overestimated.

The War Department approved the offering of correspondence courses to enemy prisoners of war and several enrolled for courses in English, Geography, and Latin. In a letter received from the camp spokesman at the Prisoner of War Camp, Papago Park, Arizona, expressing appreciation of the services rendered, he says, "All students . . . assured me of having enjoyed their studies and having gained a lot. Your method of teaching, having been new to us, has been greatly appreciated. . . . We should be glad if the American Government would permit us further enrollments from Germany."

Soon after the establishment of army convalescent hospitals near Chapel Hill, army "tours" became a regular activity. The Division was asked to make the necessary local arrangements. Aside from the fact that an outing was in itself a morale builder for men so closely confined, the tours were frequently a part of their educational program. Since many young men plan to enter or return to college after their discharge from the service, they visited the departments of Physical Education, Physics, Chemistry, and others and asked questions regarding entrance requirements and fees. During a six month period, there were an average of three such tours each week. A representative of the Division or the University Public Relations Committee accompanied each group around the campus and presented human interest stories, as well as historical data and academic information.

THE WAR INFORMATION CENTER

AGATHA BOYD ADAMS, SUPERVISOR

Several weeks before Pearl Harbor the rumor began to go around that an Information Center was to be established in the University Library—only we didn't call it a War Information Center then. "Information Center on Civilian Morale" was the first title chosen. And that change, by the way, from the restrained phrase "civilian morale" to the grim word "war" reflected the tremendous change in American attitudes during the year that was past, the change from defense to the aggression of total war. Back in those weeks before Pearl Harbor, and even immediately afterwards, there were sceptics who questioned the need for a special wartime information center in the Library. What was it for? What purpose would it serve not already adequately served by existing departments of the Library? If requests for such information came in, couldn't they be handled by the Extension Library? Even those of us who started working on the Center from the very beginning were not a bit sure just where we were going. But Charles E. Rush, University Librarian, had established such a Center in the Cleveland Public Library more than a year before. He was convinced of its usefulness and its importance. And he had the farsightedness and the enthusiasm which the rest of us lacked —at the beginning. The Information Center at Chapel Hill was actually opened the morning of December 8, 1941. Thus both Cleveland and the University of North Carolina became pioneers in establishing information centers.

What was the purpose of the Information Center? Primarily, to acquire a highly selected collection of up-to-date books, pamphlets, maps, clippings and other materials relative to the war which we were all engaged in fighting; to focus attention on this material; to make it readily accessible, easy to see, to examine, to borrow for reading; to make this material available not only to students of the University and the people of Chapel Hill, but also to anyone in the State who wanted it. Elmer Davis had challenged librarians "to see to it that the people have the facts before them. . .In the present war, as never before, this duty of librarians assumes a first and pressing importance." The War Information Center was the University Library's answer to that challenge—an answer made almost a year before Elmer Davis's appeal to American libraries was issued.

One of the first steps in establishing the Information Center was to find out what books the Library already had which were related to the present crisis. This was done before any new books were bought. Many of these already-owned books were brought out of their hiding places in the stacks and put on open shelves where everyone could see them; they were recent books on the different countries at war, our allies and our enemies, and books dealing with the history of the past twenty-five years, the failures of peace and the causes of conflict.

Another step was to write to such agencies as the British Information Services, the representatives in this country of the allied governments in exile, and many agencies interested in peace, in post-war planning, and ask to be put on their mailing list. This request bore much fruit—some days almost too much. Interesting and lively pamphlets and posters began to arrive in quantities large enough to keep the small staff busy taking care of them.

Early in December, 1941, the Information Center had been designated one of the one hundred and forty key centers of information to be sponsored in colleges and universities throughout the country by the United States Office of Education. This meant that we immediately began to receive material from the government; from the Office of Facts and Figures—later superseded by the Office of War Information; from the Office of Price Administration, from the Office of Education, from the National Resources Planning Board, and numerous other related or associated agencies. The Information Center assumed bulk and reality as the files of pamphlets filled up. We were beginning to grasp more clearly what sources of material we could count on, what kinds of information could be derived from that material, how it might be used.

The University set aside a sum of money to be used to buy new books, pamphlets, magazines, and maps for the Information Center. Month by month, that sum was used to add to the collection of fresh up-to-the-minute books about our allies, about our armed forces, and about the various intricate and far-reaching problems of global war, both at home and overseas.

The location of the Information Center helped to draw the attention of all readers to it. In the main lobby of the Library, just at the front entrance, a big V-shaped counter held the most recently received books, and such current periodicals as *Life, Fortune, The United States News, New Europe, Britain,* and news from the different governments in exile. Back of the counter were shelves of recent books. All of the material assembled here could be taken out, including the magazines and the extensive collection of pamphlets. Someone was always in attendance at the desk, to help those who wanted suggestions about reading.

Colorful and often dramatic war posters were displayed on bulletin boards around the center. Some of these were from our own government—others came from overseas, from India, from Canada, from Czechoslovakia, from Australia, from Great Britain. They were frequently changed, so that there was nearly always something new and arresting to look at. Four other bulletin boards carried the news of the day in clippings, pictures, and maps. A large scale map of the world, and another large map of the Pacific helped in locating rapidly shifting events.

The Information Center was open all day every week day including Saturday, and every evening except Saturday and Sunday. It would not have been possible to keep it open for such long hours without the aid of volunteers. Women who, when they volunteered with the Chapel Hill Office of Civilian Defense indicated a preference for work of this type, were assigned to the Information Center for duty. This group of twenty or more women disproved every objection that has ever been raised to the use of volunteers. The achievement of these volunteers maintained a very high average, and many of them experienced the thrill of satisfaction that comes from finding just the right book, or just the right answer to a request. The work of these volunteers was undoubtedly a factor in winning for the Information Center the commendation of the Carnegie Corporation. The annual report of the corporation for 1942, in speaking of the part played by libraries in the war effort, singled out the public libraries in Baltimore, Los Angeles, Denver, and New York, and then continued "The University of North Carolina, with its unusual library of war literature staffed chiefly by faculty wives and serving the entire State, is an outstanding example among the academic libraries."

The Information Center loaned books and pamphlets to those who wanted them, without any rental, serivce charge, or fine. And that went for everybody in the State of North Carolina. The morning mail might bring a request from a small public library in the western part of the State: "We are putting on an exhibit on the United Nations. Can you lend us material?" We could, and one member of the staff started collecting books, pamphlets, and posters to be lent for that exhibit. A school library wanted material on service opportunities in the armed forces. A lad already in the Naval Reserve and located in an isolated community wanted the required list of technical books for his branch. A preacher was interested especially in plans for peace; what could we send him?

Both students and faculty responded with enthusiasm to the service offered by the Information Center. Their enthusiasm and their interest suggested ways of enlarging and enriching the scope of our collection. The use of the Information Center by the campus in general amply justified the farsightedness of Mr. Rush in establishing such a collection. We endeavored to keep the collection flexible and aware of the constantly shifting needs and interests of the University, the community, and the State.

VIII
A LOOK AHEAD

A LOOK AHEAD

In the preceding chapters, the story of University Extension in action at the University of North Carolina has been presented in rather general terms. Little attempt has been made to explain in detail the services and activities or to evaluate them. An objective appraisal of University Extension might well be the subject of a special study, the result of which would unquestionably aid in planning its future growth and development. Certain trends, however, point the way toward both immediate and long-range objectives.

University policy has clearly defined the function of the University Extension Division to be chiefly administrative in nature. It has, through the years, come to be regarded as the agency of the University for the organization and promotion of educational programs, both formal and informal, not provided for in the regular budget but which could be financed through special grants or revenue-producing services. Such pioneering and experimentation, frequently in new fields of educational endeavor, has often resulted in the adoption by resident departments of new course offerings and the modification of others. The Division should, no doubt, continue to serve as a clearing house agency for the implementation of new ventures in University education, especially when these are set up to meet the needs of both resident and non-resident students.

It is assumed that there will always be a demand for off-campus courses carrying academic credit. The number of part-time, adult students has increased by the hundreds with the return of men and women who served in the armed forces and who are eligible for educational benefits provided by the "G I Bill of Rights." Extension class instruction and correspondence courses are, in many instances, the only means whereby veterans may work at home and at the same time continue their college education. The organization in all parts of the State of College Centers may prove to be one of the best means of solving the current pressures for college education from veterans and from non-veteran high school graduates. Such instruction must be closely integrated with resident instruction so that University standards will be maintained. Extension teaching has, unfortunately, been thought of by some college and university professors and administrators as being outside the realm of "academic respectability." Yet, those who have had extension teaching experience know that mature adult students, whose study is usually highly motivated, are often able students. They respond favorably to and appreciate good teaching. The quality of both extension class instruction and correspondence instruction must be second to none. Non-credit courses, likewise, must be of the highest quality since they, too, represent the University.

Other well established extension services, such as Library Extension, Community Drama, Music, Lectures, Art, High School Activities, and Short Courses and Institutes, will need to be strengthened and continued indefinitely so long as these services are adjusted to modern trends in education and changing community needs. The policy of cooperating educationally with organized groups has proven successful and should be expanded to include a greater variety of interests and organizations.

The new policy of planning off-campus work in teacher education as a part of the University's total program of teacher education is both sound and progressive. The Department of Education has a special responsibility to maintain close working relationships with the schools, the State Department of Public Instruction, and educational organizations.

It seems clearly apparent that the greatest opportunity for enlarging University services to the people lies in the direction of what may be called informal adult educational activities.

Non-credit courses, public forums, discussion groups, radio programs, reading and study guides, and greatly increased utilization of the new tools for learning such as motion pictures, film strips, recordings, and other audio-visual aids, will undoubtedly become leading forms of University Extension in the immediate future. The Institute of Government has been unusually successful in the development and use of informal methods of instruction with adult groups. Its publications and techniques of adult education with governmental officials and lawyers are indicative of the possibilities for service open to the University with other lay and professional groups.

The University of North Carolina has always identified itself with movements by citizens of the State for the improvement of the health, welfare, education, recreation, and the economic development of the people. Faculty members, students, and University alumni are frequently among the leaders of such efforts and, over the years, they have exerted a tremendous influence toward securing a higher standard of living in North Carolina. Academic freedom has been maintained, not without struggle; and freedom of speech, assembly, and publication are the priceless heritage of the institution. These freedoms must be fought for continuously if it is to be worthy of the name "University." And, in keeping them, it is of the utmost importance that the University take the initiative and participate with the people in their struggle for freedom, whether it be social, political, intellectual, or economic. If public enlightenment is the key to intelligent social action, as most of our leading thinkers proclaim it to be, then it follows that the continuous education of adults is one of the most important, if not *the* most important, function of public education. Therefore, the University with all of its resources in leadership and facilities for promoting education has a responsibility to make them available to the people, in order that they may be aided in the building of better homes, better communities, and a better world.

The Communication Center

One of the most promising recent developments in University Extension at the University of North Carolina is the Communication Center. Eventually it will include a frequency modulation educational radio station (with a state-wide network of similar stations), a motion picture production studio, a photographic laboratory, an experimental television studio, and recording studios. It will serve as a teaching as well as a production center. But when it begins broadcasting radio programs, telecasting, and distributing audio-visual aids and other media of communication to all parts of the State, and beyond, the Center will, in time, supplant many of the present forms of extension and play perhaps the leading role in providing adult educational opportunities for the people of North Carolina. The ground work is now being carefully laid for what promises to become an outstanding center in this region of the United States for the communication of ideas by means of the latest technical and scientific discoveries and mechanical aids to learning.

Workers Education

Mention has been made in Chapter VI of the beginnings of special extension services to business and industry. Almost simultaneously, there is being planned a cooperative educational program with labor. An Advisory Committee on Workers Education was appointed in 1945, consisting of representatives of the North Carolina Federation of Labor, the Congress of Industrial Organizations, the Standard Railroad Brotherhoods, and each unit of the University of North Carolina. In the spring of 1946 an Institute of Industrial Relations was set up at Chapel

A LOOK AHEAD 161

Hill, as a part of the University Extension Division, through which programs of workers education are now being conducted.

Requests from labor unions for educational services are rapidly increasing. During recent months a number of leadership training institutes have been held at the University in cooperation with various labor unions in the State and the region. There is ample evidence of a real need on the part of local union officials and members for educational assistance and for training in labor history, law, economics, collective bargaining, public speaking, parliamentary procedure, community organization, government, and recreation.

The technique of workers education calls for skilled leadership. Hence the future of this phase of University Extension will depend very largely upon the ability of the University to provide competent direction and to employ teachers who are qualified to work with labor in the local community.

Workers education is both a challenge and an opportunity to the University to serve large numbers of citizens and taxpayers through their own organizations. In general, it may be said that these groups have had little contact with their State University and that they have every right to expect it to assist them in solving their educational problems. Historically, labor has been one of the leading supporters of public education in the United States. Americans have much to learn from the experience of workers education in Great Britain where government subsidies help defray the cost of the program which is actively supported by Oxford and Cambridge Universities. Many of the leading universities in this country, including Harvard, Wisconsin, Cornell, Rutgers, and California, have conducted educational services with labor for a number of years.

At the present time, plans are being made nationally to request the federal government to appropriate funds for labor education which would be channelled through the Department of Labor to the state departments of labor and to the universities. Such a program would be for labor, in principle at least, comparable to the Agricultural Extension Service for farmers.

CULTURAL AND RECREATIONAL LIFE

Another trend of University Extension is that of greater activity and participation in the cultural and recreational life of the State. Chapel Hill has always been a center of music, art, drama, philosophy, creative writing, and natural beauty. People visit the University by the thousands each year. The Planetarium, gift of a University alumnus, John Motley Morehead, will attract thousands more and afford them unusual opportunity to see and to understand the wonders of the universe.

The imprint of the University upon the cultural and recreational life of the people is being made more significant by means of its leadership and encouragement of various state-wide activities that reach even into the remote corners of North Carolina. Notable have been the contributions of University faculty and staff members to the North Carolina Recreation Commission, the North Carolina Symphony Society, the Roanoke Island Historical Commission, the Friends of Person Hall Art Gallery, the North Carolina Library Association, the Citizens Library Movement, the North Carolina State Art Society, the North Carolina State Literary and Historical Association, the North Carolina Folklore Society, and many other organizations engaged in developing the cultural life of the State through music, art, drama, libraries, folklore, and wholesome recreational activities.

LEADERSHIP AND TEACHING MATERIALS

With the inevitable expansion of adult education programs there will fall upon the University the responsibility of assuming its share of the task of training leaders and teachers, and of preparing new and better teaching materials. There is now, and has been, a scarcity of both good teachers and literature in the field of adult education. The future of adult education calls for able administrators, teachers, writers, discussion leaders and technicians, as well as teaching aids including guide books, text books, films, recordings, film strips, and other material suitable for adults. The resident departments of the University should give immediate attention to this problem and the Extension Division should be alert in assisting communities in the training of adult education teachers and in supplying needed teaching materials.

Another challenge to University Extension is that of providing leadership in community organization for adult education. This involves the all important matter of intelligent community planning and the integration of adult education with the total educational program, and with the life of the community.

It is obvious that the University must maintain continuous relationships with state, regional, national, and international adult education organizations in order to keep our leaders informed and to share in the planning and growth of the movement.

Plans for regional training programs and for the exchange of adult education leadership among the states in the South are already under way. The services of specialists from other sections of the country will be utilized, as they have been in the past, by the University and by state and local agencies of adult education.

Research Interpretation

A new development closely related to the Extension Division and having important implications for adult education is the Division of Research Interpretation established in 1946 in the Institute for Research in Social Science. Research is significant only to the extent that it makes some contributions to the enrichment of living. The processes for systematically channelling results of research to the people who need the information generally have not been identified and used. These processes, in both their discovery and application, open a fertile field of inquiry and service for social science. This is the task to which the Division of Research Interpretation devotes its efforts.

The Division, while adhering to a prime objective of personnel training in its area of interest, features four major activities:

1. Studies are conducted to determine the accessibility and extent of use and effectiveness of various media of communication, *e.g.*, newspapers, films, magazines, radios, library services, pamphlets, personal contacts, community activities. Also, studies are developed to ascertain the best procedures for effectively contacting various socio-economic groups. Graduate asssitants are supervised in research in this field.
2. A research translation service is conducted which (a) on request, analyzes the adequacy of educational materials and suggests procedures for their improvement; (b) develops and evaluates written and visual techniques for presentation of difficult subject matter and concepts; and (c) conducts training clinics in translation techniques for personnel of public and private agencies. Graduate assistants receive experience and supervision in this field.
3. A training program in unified regional and community development is offered through collaboration with and assistance to appropriate University departments in (a) guiding a special program of study on both the graduate and undergraduate levels; (b) conducting special institutes and workshops, both on campus and off, for news-

paper editors, ministers, public health personnel, public housing officials, etc. One part of this effort involves securing in-service assistance for community leaders, *e.g.*, those mentioned above, so that a limited number of *demonstration areas* are developed. Graduate assistants receive experience and do supervised research in this field.

4. Experiments in *applied social science* are directed toward improvement of living through resource development, with special attention to some outstanding need in the area chosen. Graduate assistants also work in this field.

The Division program is set up so that qualified graduate students may, by assuming part-time staff positions, receive supervised work-experience in Division activities. Graduate study is thus combined with a specific program responsibility. In addition, a limited number of fellowships are provided for the staff assistants. The Division, while drawing widely on faculty members in other parts of the University, has a central staff including a director, three program assistants, and secretarial personnel.

"All-University" Extension

The resources of each of the three units of the University of North Carolina should be made readily available to all the people of the State. This calls for a high degree of coordination and administration of University Extension. The present Directorate of Extension has been successful in establishing general policies, in promoting cooperative relationships in extension work, and in eliminating duplication of effort. Each institution has retained autonomy of control and freedom of action within certain agreed-upon limitations and special fields of activity. There remain, however, great possibilities for united services and united action. Through careful planning and direction, the University should be able to approach local groups of people as one institution and arrange to offer "All-University" services. Certain types of extension work might be conducted more effectively and become more beneficial to the people if the services of faculty members of each unit were utilized as, for example, in a state-wide program of adult education in international relations, or a program of consumer education, or perhaps one of resource-use education.

In order that citizens living in small farm communities and rural areas may receive broader educational services from their State University, it seems highly desirable that there should be greater cooperation and coordination between the Agricultural Extension Service and the University Extension Division representing so-called general extension services. Likewise, better balanced programs of vocational and cultural or general adult education need to be worked out.

Public forums and discussion programs for farmers, industrial workers, business men and women, civic and social organizations, and other groups could be conducted in all parts of the State under University leadership and on practically any topic of public interest. The authorative information possessed by members of the faculties of the consolidated University has never been fully utilized or adequately presented to the people. This and other resources of the institution should be made available to increasingly larger numbers of citizens by means of radio programs, publications, library services, audio-visual aids, etc., as well as through personal contacts such as lectures, group discussions, conferences, class instruction, and other activities.

The opportunities for adult education, under University auspices, are limited only to the foresight, imagination, and organizing skill of administrators of University Extension. Financial considerations, important as they may be, are secondary to alert, vigorous leadership and to the cooperation of University personnel. Many adult education programs may be expected to become partially self-supporting. Others, like radio, will have to be financed (or subsidized) by either state or private funds, or both. The public has demonstrated an active interest in such educational services and a willingness to support them through both taxation and the payment of fees. Federal aid for adult education, including some forms of University Extension, is not unlikely in the near future. It therefore becomes a matter of major concern to the University to plan intelligently and rationally for the expansion and development of University Extension if this function of the University is to be unimpaired and its service to the people of the State is to become more significant socially, economically, and spiritually.

INDEX

Adams, Agatha Boyd, iii, 51, 53, 150
Advisory service, dramatic art, 68; music, 76; teaching, 97
Agricultural Extension Service, 166
Alderman, Edwin A., 12, 13
All-State High School Music Course, 43, 75-76, 99
Alumni, work of, 11, 12, 13
American Association for Adult Education, 100, 103
American Council of Learned Societies, 47
American Legion, 46
American Red Cross. *See* Red Cross, Southeastern Area American
Art, 59-62; traveling exhibitions of, 59-61; contests in, 99; *See also* Folklore Council; North Carolina Congress of Parents and Teachers; North Carolina State Department of Public Instruction
Art, Department of, 27, 29, 61, 99
Athletic Association. *See* North Carolina State High School Athletic Association
Athletic contests. *See* North Carolina State High School Athletic Association
Athletic Department. *See* Physical Education and Athletics, Department of
Audio-Visual Education, Bureau of, 62-64, 103, 139, 149
Aycock, Charles B., 12, 13
Aycock Cup, 65

Bankers' Conference, 45
Bar Association Seminar. *See* State Bar Association Seminar
Basic English, 127
Battle, Kemp Plummer, 11
Blackwell, Gordon, 111, 116
Bond, Marjorie, 53
Bond, Richmond P., 53
Boy Scout Jubilee, 47
Boy Scouts of America, 47
Boys' State, 46
Branson, E. C., 16, 78, 111
Bulletin of the North Carolina Council for the Social Studies, 82
Bull's Head Bookshop, 54, 55
Business Services and Research, Bureau of, iv, 109

Carnegie Endowment for International Peace, 101, 102, 105, 126
Carolina Dramatic Association, 46, 68, 69, 71, 138

Carolina Institute of International Relations, 46, 139
Carolina Playmakers, 3, 17, 138-39; of the air, 71, 85
Chase, Harry Woodburn, 17, 18
Civilian Morale Service, 7, 142-43. *See also* War Information Center
Coaching School for Athletic Directors and Coaches, 43
Coates, Albert, iv, 119
Cobb, Mary Louisa, 30
Coker, W. C., 17
Commerce, School of, 44, 45, 47, 82, 109
Commercial and Industrial Relations, Bureau of, 18, 82
Commission on Teacher Education, report of, 33
Commonwealth Fund, 105, 128, 129
Communication Center, 8, 130, 160
Community Drama, Bureau of, 18, 67-71, 96. *See also* Carolina Dramatic Association; Carolina Playmakers; Dramatic Festival; radio
Community Music, Bureau of, 18, 75. *See also* Music, Department of
Community Organization, Bureau of, 18
Community services. *See* Services to communities
Conferences, 42-48, 146-48
Conservation of Marriage and the Family, 43, 118-19
Southern Conference on Education, 44
Bankers', 45
Health Education, 47
North Carolina Scholastic Press Association, 47
Rural Education, 47
Safety, 47
School Librarians, 47
Carolina Dramatic Association, 70
on recreation, 86
on public forums, 92
Child Health, 96
Work Conference on Optimum Production, 112
Regionalism in World Economics, 116
Lecture-Seminar-Conference on the Education of the American Negroes and the African Natives, 116
Labor in the War, 147
See also conventions, institutes, short courses, symposia, workshops
Connor, R. D. W., 53
Contests, debating, 4, 14, 15, 65, 140; ath-

INDEX

letic, 66; academic, 67; art, 99; journalism, 99
Conventions, American Chemical Society, 92; National Academy of Science, 92; North Carolina Photographers Association, 92; Post Office Clerks and Letter Carriers, 92. *See also* conferences, short courses, institutes, symposia, workshops
Correspondence and Class Instruction, Bureau of, 18
Correspondence instruction, 17, 18, 28-30, 86, 144-46
Couch, W. T., 131, 132, 133
County Public Welfare Superintendents and Directors, Institute for, 44
Creative Music Course, 43
Credit, correspondence courses, 28; extension classes, 26, 27, 68, 75; short courses, 43, 96
Curriculum study by English teachers, 73

Debate Handbook, 66
Debating. *See* North Carolina High School Debating Union
Dental courses. *See* Post-Graduate Medical and Dental Courses
Design and improvement of school grounds, 17, 18
Dey, William, M., 48
Dialectic Literary Society, 14, 65
Directorate of Extension, 21, 165
Directors' Conference of the Carolina Dramatic Association, 70
Division of Public Welfare and Social Work of the Graduate School, 44, 47
Dogwood Festival, 110
Douglass, Harl R., 37
Drama. *See* Community Drama, Bureau of
Dramatic Art, Department of, 44, 69, 71, 83, 100; high school course in, 44, 100
Dramatic Festival, 46, 69-71, 138
Duke University, 118, 127

Education, Department of, 38, 43, 44, 47, 75, 97, 158
Educational information service, 17, 18
Educational Research and Service, Bureau of, 36-37
Engineering, Science, and Management War Training, 7, 143-44
English, Department of, 43, 71
English for Latin Americans, courses in, 43, 129
English extension service, 71-73
English Institute. *See* High School English Institute
English Teacher, 73, 82

Extension Bureau Circulars, 80, 81
Extension, Bureau of, 4, 7, 16-17, 51, 66, 74, 137
Extension classes, 18, 25, 30, 32, 34, 86
Extension Leaflets, 79, 80-81
Extension Lectures, Bureau of, 17, 18
Extension Library Service, 28, 51-55, 102
Extension News. See University of North Carolina Extension News
Extension Series, 79

Faculty Committee on Extension, 15, 16, 51
Faculty cooperation, extension classes, 26, 27
correspondence instruction, 30
preparation of study outlines, 53
lecture service, 74
radio, 82, 84, 141
Parent-Teacher work, 94
federal programs, 104
research interpretation, 114
Inter-American Institute, 126
University Press, 131, 133
Civilian Morale Service, 142
prisoner of war programs, 149
Family, Conference on Conservation of Marriage and the. *See* Marriage and the Family, Annual Conference on
Family Service Association of America. *See* Regional Institute of Family Service Association of America
Federal agencies, 7, 98-99, 104, 138-54
See also Office of the Coordinator of Inter-American Affairs, 101, 105, 126, 141
Office of Price Administration, 7
Office of War Information, 7, 139
United States Armed Forces Institute, 7, 144-46
United States Employment Service, 103
United States Office of Education, 77, 103, 109, 128, 143
Federal Emergency Relief Administration, 98-99
Filene Good Will Fund, 105
Films, 63, 64, 102, 117, 128, 139-40, 149
Folk Music, Institute of, 110
Folklore Council, 110-11
Frazer, Keener C., 102
French House, 43
Friederich, W. G., 116

General Education Board, 105
General Information Service, 16
Geology, Department of, 48
Good Roads Institute, 17
Graham, E. K., 15, 16, 52

INDEX 171

Graham, Frank Porter, 4, 19; inaugural address of, 4, 19-20
Green, Elizabeth Lay, 53
Green, Paul, 53
Grumman, Russell M., 19
Grumman, Vida Church, iv
Groves, Ernest R., 118-19
Groves, Gladys Hoagland, 119

Hamilton, J. G. deR., 17
Hampton Institute, 117
Health Education Conference, 47
Hibbard, Addison, 53
High School Course in Dramatic Art, 100
High School Debating and Athletics, Bureau of, 18
High School Debating Union. *See* North Carolina High School Debating Union
High School English Institute, 43, 72-73
High School Music Course. *See* All-State High School Music Course
High School relations, 4, 66. *See also* Audio-Visual Education, Bureau of; All-State High School Music Course; Community Drama, Bureau of; contests; English in Extension; High School Course in Dramatic Art
History, academic contest in, 67

In-service teacher education, 5, 25, 27, 30-39, 97; suggested experiment, 34-37
Institute for Research in Social Science, iv, 8, 43, 44, 111-19, 163
Institute of Folk Music, 110
Institute of Government, iv, 44, 46, 47, 111, 119-25, 159
Institute of Industrial Relations, 160-61
Institute of International Relations. *See* Carolina Institute of International Relations
Institutes, 42-48, 146
  English, 43, 72
  County Public Welfare Superintendents and Directors, 44
  Public Health Dentistry, 44
  Management of Childrens' Institutions, 44
  Public Welfare, 44
  Public Welfare Case Workers, 44
  Annual Newspaper, 46
  International Relations, 46, 139
  Parent-Teacher, 46, 94
  Linguistic, 47
  Professional Relations, 47
  Family Service Association, 47
  Science Teachers', 47
  on recreation, 86

Business and Professional Women's Clubs, 92
Textile Workers Union of America, 92
North Carolina Federation of Women's Clubs, 92
Southern Regional Development and the Social Sciences, 113
Population Research, Regional Research, and the Measurement of Regional Development, 114
for city, county, state and federal officials, 124
for public affairs committees, 124
for teachers of civics, 124
Labor in National Defense, 147
How Labor can Help Safeguard America's Wage Dollar, 147
Training Institutes for Labor Unions, 161
See also, conferences, conventions, short courses, symposia, workshops
Insurance School, 45
Inter-American Institute, 43, 103, 105, 125-29
Intersession Summer Sessions for Teachers, 44
Ivey, John E., 113

Jocher, Katherine, iv, 111
Jones, Howard Mumford, 53
Journalism, Department of, 46, 47, 99, 141
Joyner, James Y., 13

Kelling, Lucile, 53
Koch, Frederick H., 68, 138

Language Arts Bulletin, 73
Latin, academic contest in, 67
Latin America, lectures on, 101
Latin American Summer School, 126-28
Laura Spelman Rockefeller Foundation, 105
Law, School of, 47
Lawrence, Elizabeth, 53
Leavitt, Sturgis E., iv, 125, 126
Lecture-Seminar-Conference on the Education of the American Negroes and the African Natives, 116-18
Lectures, 15, 17, 74-75, 101, 141
Librarians' Conference. *See* School Librarians' Conference
Library Extension Service, iv, 18, 51-55, 94
Library of the Bureau of Audio-Visual Education, 64
Library Extension Publication. See University of North Carolina Library Extension Publication
Library Science, School of, 47
Lingle, Mrs. T. W., 52

Loram, Charles T., 117
Love, Cornelia Spencer, 53
Ludington, John, 34

McCall, Adeline, 53
McIntosh, C. E., iii, 11
McIver, Charles D., 12, 13
Master's degree credits earned by extension, 32
Marriage and the Family, Annual Conference on, 43, 118-19
Mathematics, academic contest in, 67
Medical instruction, 17. *See also* Post-Graduate Medical and Dental Courses
Meyer, Harold D., 85
Mims, Edwin, 15
Morrison, Roy W., iii, 30
Municipal Information and Research, Bureau of, 18
Municipal Reference, 17
Music, Department of, 43, 44, 75, 76, 83, 99, 110, 111
Music in extension, 75-76, 110. *See also*, All-State High School Music Course, 43, 75-76, 99; Folklore Council 110-11; University Glee Clubs, 76; radio, 82-85, 140

National foundations, 104, 105. *See also* Commonwealth Fund; Carnegie Endowment for International Peace; National organizations
National organizations, cooperation with, 47, 102-6. *See also*, American Council of Learned Societies; American Association for Adult Education; Boy Scouts of America; national foundations
National University Extension Association, 2, 102
News Letter See University of North Carolina News Letter
Newspaper Institute, 46
Noble, M. C. S., 17
Non-credit courses, 27, 32, 35, 38-42, 45; for doctors, 39-41; for dentists, 41-42
North Carolina Association for Certified Public Accountants, 48
North Carolina Association of Insurance Agents, 46
North Carolina Association of Real Estate Agents, 47
North Carolina Bankers' Association, 45
North Carolina Bar Association, 47
North Carolina Club Yearbook, 16
North Carolina College Conference, 5
North Carolina College for Women. *See* Woman's College of the University of North Carolina

North Carolina Commerce and Industry, 82
North Carolina Congress of Parents and Teachers, 5, 46, 62, 93-95
North Carolina Dental Society, 41
North Carolina Department of Highways, 47
North Carolina Education Association, 5, 36-47; recommendations on off-campus teachers education, 38; department of school librarians, 47; department of science teachers, 47; department of English teachers, 72-73
North Carolina Federation of Women's Clubs, 52, 59, 61
North Carolina High School Debating Union, 4, 14, 15, 65, 140
North Carolina Lecture-Institute Program, 101
North Carolina Photographers Association, 48
North Carolina Press Association, 46
North Carolina Recreation Commission, 87
North Carolina Scholastic Press Institute, 99
North Carolina State Board of Health, 17, 39, 96-97
North Carolina State College of Agriculture and Engineering, 21, 116
North Carolina State Department of Public Instruction, 5, 12, 31, 33, 37, 47, 73, 76, 77, 96-100, 143, 158
North Carolina State Federation of Women's Clubs, 52, 59, 61
North Carolina State High School Athletic Association, 66
North Carolina Symphony Society, 110
Nursing Education, courses in, 43

Odum, Howard W., 111, 113, 117
Office of the Coordinator of Inter-American Affairs, 101, 105, 126, 141
Office of Price Administration, 7
Office of War Information, 7, 139
Orange County Art Project, 61

Parent-Teacher Association. *See* North Carolina Congress of Parents and Teachers
Parent-Teacher Handbook, 94
Parent-Teacher Institute, 46. *See also* North Carolina Congress of Parents and Teachers
Patterson, A. H., 15
Person Hall Art Gallery, 3
Personnel Management, Workshop in, 44
Philanthropic Literary Society, 14, 65
Photography, courses in, 43
Photography, School of, 47

INDEX

Physical Education and Athletics, Department of, 43
Physically Handicapped, courses for teachers of, 43
Physics, academic contest in, 67
Physics, Department of, 43, 47
Pierson, W. W., 52
Portuguese House, 44
Post-Graduate Medical and Dental Courses, 39-42, 96
Potter, Russell, 53
Pratt, Joseph Hyde, 17
Prisoners of war, 146, 149-50
Professional Relations Institute, 47
Public Discussion, 16, 18. See also Public forums
Public forums, 77-78, 103, 142, 166
Public Health Dentistry, Institute of, 44
Public Health Nursing Course, 44
Public Health, School of, 43, 44
Public schools. See Services to the public schools
Public Welfare Institute, 44
Publications, 78-82; English teachers, 72-73; Extension Library, 80; Bureau of Commercial and Industrial Relations, 82; of social science teachers, 82; Bureau of Recreation, 85-86; Institute for Research in Social Science, 113-14; Institute of Government, 124

Radio, 82-85, 140; forums, 143, 160; cooperation with, Music Department, 76, 83, 141; Dramatic Art Department, 141; Department of Journalism, 141; Southern Council on International Relations, 141
Rankin, E. R., 16, 17
Rankin, Dr. W. S., 39
Raper, C. L., 17
Real Estate School, 47
Record. See University of North Carolina Record
Recreation, 85-87
Red Cross, Southeastern Area American, 100
Regional Institute of the Family Service Association of America, 47
Regional organizations, cooperation with, 100-2. See also Southeastern Folklore Society, 111; Southern Council on International Relations, 141
Regionalism in World Economics, Conference on, 116
Report, Faculty Committee on Extension, 15; Director Snell, 18-19
Research Interpretation, Division of, 8, 113, 119, 163-65
Roberson, Nellie, 52, 53

Romance Languages, Department of, 43, 44, 47, 48
Rosenstengel, W. E., 34
Rosenwald Fund, 105
Royster, J. F., 53
Royster, Mrs. J. F., 53
Rural Education Conference, 47
Rural Social-Economics, Department of, 16
Rush, Charles E., 142, 151, 154

Safety Conference, 47
Saturday classes, experiment in, 34, 44
School-Health Coordinating Service, 96
School Librarians' Conference, 47
Schools. See Services to the public schools
Services to communities:
  extension courses, 25
  art, 61
  audio-visual aids, 62-64
  dramatic art, 67-70
  lectures, 74-75, 86
  music, 75-76
  radio, 76, 78, 82-85
  University glee clubs, 76
  public forums, 77-78
  recreation, 85, 86
  Parent-Teacher Associations, 94
  international relations, 101
Services to the public schools:
  debating, 4, 14, 15, 65-66
  library, 51-55
  art, 59-62, 94, 98, 99
  teacher training, 61-64, 71, 75, 97
  audio-visual aids, 62-64
  athletic contests, 66
  academic contests, 67
  dramatic art, 67-70, 100
  curriculum planning, 73
  music, 75-76, 99
  publications, 99
Sewerage Works Operators, Short Course for, 44
Short courses:
  Coaching School for Athletic Directors and Coaches, 43
  English for Latin Americans, 43
  Teachers of the Physically Handicapped, 43
  Nursing Education, 43
  Photography, 43
  Creative Music, 43, 76
  French House, 43
  High School Music, 44
  High School Dramatic Art, 44
  Inter-session Summer Session for Teachers, 44
  Portuguese House, 44
  Public Health Nursing, 44

Sewerage Works Operators, 44
Insurance School, 45
Real Estate School, 47
Photography, 47
 in recreation, 86
 at Blue Ridge, 98
 for teachers of home nursing, 100
 for swimming instructors, 100. *See also* conferences, conventions, institutes, symposia, workshops
Short Courses and Institutes, Bureau of, 18
Smith, Dr. W. H., 40
Snell, Chester D., 17, 18, 19
Social and Economic Surveys, Bureau of, 16, 18
Social Studies Institute, 44
Social Work Institute for Public Welfare Case Workers, 44
Sociology, Department of, 47
South and World Affairs, 101
Southeastern Association for Adult Education, 100
Southeastern Folklore Society, 100, 111
Southern Conference on Education, 44
Southern Council on International Relations, 100, 101-2; 141
Southern Regional Development, Institute on, 113, 114
Spanish, academic contest in, 67
Speaker service. *See* Lectures
Spearman, Dale, 53
Spearman, Walter, 53
Stacy, M. H., 15
State Bar Association Seminar, 47
State Board of Health. *See* North Carolina State Board of Health
State College of Agriculture and Engineering. *See* North Carolina State College of Agriculture and Engineering
State Department of Highway Engineering, 17
State Department of Public Instruction. *See* North Carolina State Department of Public Instruction
State Inspector of High Schools, 14
State Literary and Historical Commission, 15
State Normal and Industrial College. *See* Woman's College of the University of North Carolina
State organizations, cooperation with, 42-48, 93-100. *See also*
  North Carolina Congress of Parents and Teachers
  North Carolina State Department of Public Instruction

North Carolina State High School Athletic Association
North Carolina High School Debating Union
North Carolina Federation of Women's Clubs
North Carolina Recreation Commission
Study outlines, 53. *See also University of North Carolina Library Extension Publication*
Stringfield, Lamar, 110
Symposium on Accounting and Taxation, 48
Symposia: Accounting and Taxation, 48; Consumer in Wartime, 148. *See also* conference, conventions, institutes, short courses, workshops

Tar Heel Banker, 45
Teacher certification, 26, 27, 97
Teachers' institutes, 12
Tours, foreign, 48; transcontinental, 48; glee club, 76; playmakers, 138; army, 150
Trabue, M. R., 37

United States Armed Forces Institute, 7, 144-46
United States Employment Service, 103
United States Office of Education, 77, 103, 109, 128, 143
University Conference on Population Research, Regional Research, the Measurement of Regional Development, 114-16
University Extension in Wartime, 7, 137-54
University Glee Clubs, 76
University News Bureau, 46
University of North Carolina Extension Bulletin, 74, 79-80, 130
University of North Carolina Extension News, 81
University of North Carolina Library Extension Publication, 52, 80
University of North Carolina News Letter, 2, 16, 78-79
University of North Carolina Press, iv, 111, 112, 117, 129-33
University of North Carolina Record, 79, 81

Valentine, Mrs. Charles, 55
Venable, Francis P., 15
Veterans education, 8
Visual Instruction, Bureau of. *See* Audio-Visual Instruction, Bureau of

Walker, N. W., 14, 15, 17, 51, 97
War Information Center, iv, 7, 76, 150-54
War Manpower Commission, 7
Wartime activities. *See* University Extension in Wartime
Williams, L. A., 17
Wilson, Louis R., iv, 13, 14, 15, 16, 39, 51, 52, 97, 131, 133
Wilson, Thomas J., iv, 129
Winter Summer School. *See* Latin American Summer School
Winslow, Rex, iv, 109

Woman's College of the University of North Carolina, 12, 59, 60, 95, 139
Work Conference on Optimum Production, 112-13
Workers education, 160-61
Workshops: personnel management, 44; Junior Red Cross, 92, 100; recreation, 86. *See also* conferences, conventions, institutes, short courses, symposia
Wynn, Earl, 85

Yale University, 117
Youth services, 87

www.ingramcontent.com/pod-product-compliance
Lightning Source LLC
Chambersburg PA
CBHW030113010526
44116CB00005B/221